H. C. Moolenburgh, M.D.

A Handbook of Angels

Translated from the Dutch
by Amina Marix-Evans

Saffron Walden
The C. W. Daniel Company Limited

First published in Great Britain by
The C. W. Daniel Company Limited
1 Church Path, Saffron Walden, Essex, England

Reprinted 1988
Reprinted 1990
Reprinted 1991
Reprinted 1992
Reprinted 1993

Originally published by
Uitgeverij Ankh-Hermes, Deventer, The Netherlands
under the title *Engelen*

ISBN 0 85207 169 8

Set in English Times by
MS Typesetting, Castle Camps, Cambridge
and printed by
Hillman Printers (Frome) Ltd, Frome, Somerset.

Contents

List of illustrations

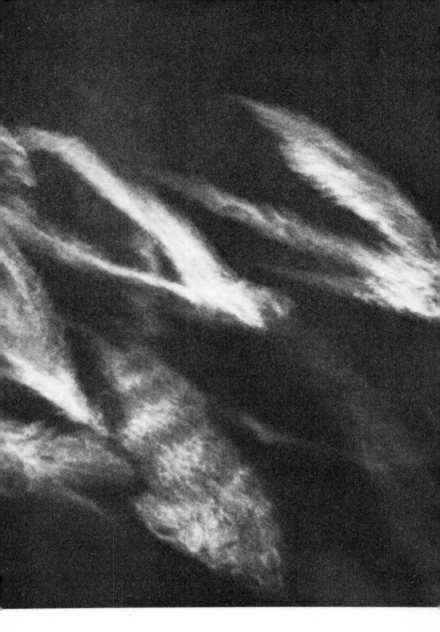

2   The play of shapes in the clouds

Introduction

In 1981 a sermon was given in Leiden in which the minister called angels a 'forgotten group'. This is an extremely striking and yet accurate remark.

The book lying in front of you is an attempt to recall this forgotten group into the memory of people. I believe this is a good cause for we read so much these days about demons, exorcism, Apocalyptic threats and other matters concerning the underworld that we are inclined to forget that an enormous 'upper world' stretches out above us. A world which is also still extremely active, and is increasingly beginning to intrude on us.

In chapter one I describe my survey of 400 people, through which I tried to gain some insight as to how we think about angels these days. The results I can only describe as spectacular.

After this I try to make it clear to the reader that the word 'angel' is really a collective name for a great variety of different groups of spiritual beings. A description of these beings has been formulated, based on the large amount of data on angels brought together over the last three thousand years.

Here I am not really primarily concerned with facts of historic interest. I want to examine with you whether, in our modern technocratic society, angels are still conceivable, and whether they could still have a task and a function in the light of present-day understanding. Thus I endeavour to marry present-day data with extremely ancient sources. Perhaps it will become apparent that though we may have forgotten this group, it has not forgotten us, but is busily returning to human consciousness on a gigantic scale. The return of the angels to human consciousness could be one of the greatest surprises of the twentieth century.

If you have any experience of Angels I would love to hear from you. Please write to me care of Uitgeverij Ankh-Hermes bv, Postbus 125, 7400 AC Deventer, Holland.

1. An Angel on your Path

What could have moved me in 1982 to start on a survey of experiences with angels? It was one of those impulses which cannot be explained logically. One day I was still living an ordinary life — to whatever extent life can be normal — the next day I was in the midst of it all.

After a consultation I asked each patient, 'Would you permit me, purely for private research purposes, to put a couple of questions to you as I am making a survey?'

The response was always one of benevolent aquiescence. 'Here is the first question: Do you have a particular religious affiliation?' This question was quickly answered.

Then I went on with, 'Now follows the question with which the survey is concerned. Have you ever in your life seen an angel?'

The reader should not imagine that it was easy to ask this question. A kind of false shame came over me each time I was about to ask it and at times I would have palpitations. I found it more difficult to put the question to men than to women, though I'm not really sure why that should be. Perhaps women these days have preserved more feeling for wonder. In any case, I kept a sharp eye on my patients so as to observe their own reaction to the question. And what was at first no more than a sort of anxious watching of the patient grew quickly into keen interest, during which I could forget myself. Because the reactions were so varied and so colourful I felt overcome by astonishment again and again. I am not talking about the actual answers, but of the emotional reactions such as astonishment, fear, bursting into laughter and the like.

It quickly became clear to me that I wasn't asking a non-committal question; the question shocked people. Asking questions about experiences with angels in the twentieth century appeared to be just as shocking as asking questions about sexual experiences in the nineteenth.

I would like to begin by giving you a summary of the reactions. The number of people to whom I put the question about angels was four hundred.

The reason for asking about religious affiliation first was in fact my own diffidence. I wanted some sort of lead to the real enquiry and therefore chose the question about religion, since that indicated the area into which we were about to move.

Later on this appeared to be a good approach, for links existed between religion and the emotional responses to the question. The reaction which occurred most frequently was one of deep contemplation. Sixty-five people, that is 16% of the total, reacted in this manner. And that is strange.

Imagine that I had asked four hundred people, 'Have you seen your mother in the last month?' They would have given me a quick 'Yes' or 'No' by way of an answer. Or, suppose I had asked them, 'Have you ever seen a living mammoth?', then the answer would have been an immediate 'No'.

A quick answer can be given to questions about matters which are clearly either possible or impossible. Why then the deep deliberation? Surely a person knows whether or not he has ever seen an angel? However these people continually gave me the impression that they were trying to remember something. Something that had escaped them only a moment before, as if they had been asked to name the children they had been with in the first class of their nursery school.

Did these people have a deep memory of angels? A memory not available to their everyday awareness but that nonetheless stirred some deeper level of consciousness? In the same way that the mood of a dream can influence your waking life even when you have forgotten the content of it?

Each time that deep contemplation surprised me anew, especially when, after some time the considered answer came, 'No, I've never seen an angel.' Of these sixty-five people, sixty-four eventually answered in the negative.

The group of 'contemplators' was followed by the second-largest group of forty-five people with a totally different reaction. They actually burst out laughing. In fact, 11% of those surveyed were highly amused, but it wasn't sneering or scornful laughter. No, it was free and cheerful, as if to say, 'Hey, that's actually possible, how nice.'

It is quite interesting to see how the people who laughed were spread out over various religious beliefs. Sixteen were agnostic, thirteen Roman Catholic, eleven Protestant and five were members of one sect or another. A quite reasonable distribution of the volley of laughter.

Here we should note that 153 of those surveyed, i.e. 38.25% of the total, had no particular religious affiliation, even though they constituted 38% of the hearty laughers. Thus they are well-represented in the cheerful group. Apparently a good many agnostics find the angel question far from absurd. They reward it with bright amusement.

What could that mean? I am inclined to explain it by saying that when you ask someone about his religious affiliation and he answers, 'I haven't got one', that his answer doesn't presuppose that he also dismisses the other, mysterious world. Agnosticism is not always the same as being closed to the world of mystery, any more, than religious people will always say that heaven is a reality.

The third large group, after the contemplators and the laughers, was the matter-of-fact group, of which there were forty-three. They found the question completely normal, on the same level as their being asked what brand of coffee they usually drank. Were these simply people who were no longer surprised by anything in this life? Or were angels simply a matter-of-fact reality? I just don't know.

Maurice Nicoll, the brilliant pupil of Gurdjieff and Ouspensky, says that you can divide people into those with, and those without, a feeling for the mysterious. Those who do have that feeling realize a question, a teaching or a story is concerned with another dimension. Those who lack that feeling translate every event in life as a phenomenon of the world as perceived by their five senses. The most striking example of this was the first person I interviewed. 'Have you ever seen an angel?'

'Certainly! An extremely beautiful one!' Can you imagine my bewilderment when I got such an answer after all the difficulties felt when first asking the angel question?

I asked very cautiously, 'What was it like?'

This charming lady looked at me, amazed at my lack of comprehension, and said, 'Last night on television!'

Directly after this last group came two equally large groups of thirty-seven people each — about 9% of the total for each group. The one group of thirty-seven reacted anywhere from being astonished to being amazed. Of these people eighteen were religious and nineteen were not.

Those with a religion were divided as follows: ten Roman Catholics, seven Protestants and one Rosicrucianist. The astonishment was about the fact that I could ask such a question seriously. 'How is that possible?' 'Surely that's impossible?' etc. If one of the Church's Articles of Faith, namely the belief in angels, becomes just as real as the existence of the baker's shop on the corner, many people would find it difficult to accept.

Everyone remembers from their schooldays what happened when you didn't know the answer to a question. To gain time you said, 'I believe . . .' whereupon the teacher said, 'Believing is what you do in church.'

That remark seems to be very much to the point, as it also

14

includes the idea that, 'Outside the church you should only believe what your senses tell you.' Mixing Articles of Faith and everyday practice becomes too difficult for most people.

The members of the second group of thirty-seven people began to radiate friendliness. As if I had just told them that their children were really exceptional people. They seemed to feel themselves confirmed in something they had already thought. That reaction often made me think of a remark made by my friend Bert, who is a clergyman. He once said to me, 'Look, when those people hear me talk about religion they think it's normal, since that's what I'm being paid for. But when they hear you talk about it, it makes a much greater impression since you, as a doctor, don't have to talk about it!'

The next group consisted of nineteen people. These were the ones who reacted in a negative way. Their reactions were shock, annoyance, suspicion and disapproval.

If one were to think that all these were people without religion that would be far from the truth. Nine were religious, ten were not. Five of these people belonged to the Dutch Reformed Church and showed annoyance, suspicion or fear. A Lutheran began to weep angrily and one Catholic became very disapproving. The remaining two of the nine religious people were Jehovah's Witnesses who said condescendingly that a human being couldn't see any such thing. I have included them in the negative reactions since this was said in a clearly correcting tone of voice. If I mention here that of the 400 people questioned, 82 (20.5%) were Roman Catholics and 50 (12.5%) were members of the Dutch Reformed Church, and we see that five Reformed and one Catholic reacted in a negative way, then it would seem that a Catholic can cope better with an angel than a member of the Reformed Church. It could be worthwhile checking this discovery on a much larger group of people. The numbers in this survey are too small; at the most it can indicate only a specific direction.

Nine of those questioned showed a heart-warming reaction. 'My husband (or wife) is an angel.' One man became so moved at this that he began to cry. Two of the nine turned it into a joke, as do so many Dutch people when they want to hide their real feelings. 'She's sitting right here,' as they point with their thumb over their shoulder to their other half. And one of those two adds, 'Though now and then she is a damned nuisance!'

I learned a lot from this group of nine. One person can be an angel for another in the course of this heavy journey through life. 'No,' said one little old lady from Amsterdam, 'No, I've never seen an angel, but I have a neighbour who is an absolute treasure.' All said in the local dialect.

And then in your mind's eye you see this neighbour. A bowl of soup when you are ill, a seat at the family table for Christmas dinner, popping in to see if everything is all right. If we were to become more aware of the way people see other people as angels, perhaps we would make more use of our latent possibilities.

A Roman poet said, 'Man is a wolf to man.' Well, it is patently clear that one man eats another in the jungle of life. Fortunately there is a very positive counterpart to this cynical Roman's remark which says, 'Man is an angel to man.'

As long as we are alive we can choose how we will relate to other people, and that is already very exceptional. It indicates the very special place of man in creation.

A real wolf remains a real wolf, but a human being can be both a wolf in sheep's clothing and a sheep in wolf's clothing. In the latter case we would speak of a rough diamond. What was remarkable was that amongst all these friendly, interested, serious or laughing people there was only one solitary person who reacted with exaltation. As if she were the possessor of a Higher Knowledge not available to ordinary mortals. However, she had never seen an angel.

From this you can see that we Dutch have little inclination to exaltation. The Dutchman stands with both feet planted firmly in the clay and doesn't easily loose his head — unless it is a match between Ajax and Feyenoord.

I discovered this very clearly once when I was in America. A healing service was being held by a well-known evangelist and all the believers stood with both hands raised to heaven, some 5000 people in all. It was an impressive sight. Suddenly I noticed a man whose hands hung down by his sides, one individual amongst a sea of people waving their upstretched hands. That man was myself. That is why the follow-up of this survey is so impressive. If a Dutchman experiences something out of the ordinary, it must be really clear or else he simply will not believe it. To round off the survey: there were quite a few other reactions, such as hesitation, embarrassment, excitement and similar responses. For instance, nineteen people reacted by showing great interest:

'Goodness, I'd like to know more!'

'Do people ever see angels?'

Twenty people reacted in a co-operative way, 'No, never an angel but I did . . .', then came a story that had something to do with the world of mystery, and I will be coming back to this later.

Fourteen people reacted very decisively. They gave an immediate answer. Usually 'No.'

And ten reacted very seriously, this being a question not to be taken lightly. Almost a question that required formal dress. I have differentiated between them and the con-templators because they gave immediate answers. The remainder of the people reacted in very divergent ways which cannot be brought into any particular group. If I put all of this together in a list we see:

Emotional reactions to the angel question

Deep contemplation	16.25%
Spontaneous laughter	11.25%
Matter-of-fact	10.75%
Astonished	9.25%
Radiant	9.25%
Interested	4.75%
Co-operative	5.00%
Negative	4.75%
Decisive	3.50%
Serious	2.50%
'My partner'	2.25%
Other reactions	20.50%

Summing up, one can say that the question about angels often calls up emotions; at least three people burst out crying. For the majority of those questioned (89%), it was not a superficial question; neither for the religious nor for those without religion. I have deliberately gone very deeply into all this. Western man is not quite as materialistic as many people think. He is forced to live in a world where matters are considered and organised in a rational and logical way. But scratch the varnish of rationality just a little and, even in this century, man is found to be intimately tied to the world of mystery.

Now I go on to deal with the answers people gave. To my astonishment, not only emotional reactions came up, but also a great many spontaneous stories which had nothing to do with angels, though they did concern the mysterious world which lies constantly just around the corner.

No less than sixty-eight of those 400 people had had strange experiences, varying from a strong feeling of being guided through dangerous situations to contact with members of their families who had died, visions and out-of-body experiences. I hasten to add that this concerns only spontaneous phenomena, and not happenings caused by spiritualist seances, the use of drugs or exercises designed to alter states of consciousness. Nor did I ask for these stories; people came up with them spontaneously because they apparently felt that my question was related to their particular extraordinary experience.

It seemed to me that for many this tangible world was not the only reality, and that the materialistic outlook propagated with so much energy is more the fantasy of a small group of intellectuals than a power which has conquered humanity by force.

Moreover, of the sixty-eight people who had remarkable experiences, thirty-five had no religious convictions. Being a member (or not) of a church did not give any indication as to whether people believed in a world other than the one in which they lived. Another world, which, once experienced, removed all fear of death. Thus, one of my patients tells me the following story:

'After work I popped in to see my next-door neighbour for a drink; she was a wise old lady, and I enjoyed talking to her. Suddenly I became unwell and felt as if I was tumbling into an enormous pit. I tried to climb out.

Meanwhile my neighbour had, with great difficulty, laid me on the sofa. Because she had seen several people die in the course of her life, she was convinced I was dead, and immediately phoned a doctor. Meanwhile, I was suddenly standing beside myself, next to my own head. I could see that my eyes were glazed and I thought, "Is that me? Hah! that's nothing. The yellow colour, that sweaty face, those glazed eyes. That thing lying there is awful, I hate it."

I felt then in my feet that my "self" was returning to its shell. It started to move. Then I opened my eyes and I was laid on a stretcher. Later on, my neighbour confirmed that everything had been exactly as I had seen it, and the heart specialist thought that for a while I had been clinically dead.

Since then I have never been afraid of death.'

And then I realised that I had asked this man if he had ever seen an angel and he had answered, 'Not me.' If I hadn't paused for a moment this story would never have come out.

Another man had broken his neck and had ended up in a ditch. In a flash he saw his whole life go by and then it was as if he were looking over a fence behind which everything was at peace. I would like to refer the reader to that beautiful painting by Hieronymus Bosch called 'The Prodigal Son'. A man with a large pack on his back has left a tumble-down house and is approaching a fence behind which can be seen a beautiful grey-green hilly landscape. Wertheim Aymes explains that we see here a man standing on the threshold of death. Several people have told me about the landscape lying just beyond that threshold to death. Actually I will not go any further into these stories because they only marginally relate to my survey on experiences with angels. They certainly tell of that other world, but not of those wonderful messengers who, from time to time, cross over from that world into ours. So now to the question at the heart of the matter, 'Have you ever seen an angel?'

One of my patients said, 'An Injun, doctor! Sure I seen one, in a Wild West Show once.' So strange is that question about angels that it was sometimes translated into something more common or would even cause temporary deafness.

'A what, doctor?'

'An angel!'

As I said, I had to overcome something each time in order to put that question. Was I afraid of being regarded as 'not all there'? Was something holding me back? Yet more and more the survey took hold of me, especially when I was confronted with the totally unexpected fact that people answered with a 'Yes' time and again. I really had not expected that. My preconceived opinion had been that the average Western person was so materialistic that encounters with angels were impossible.

But preconceived opinions are dangerous and mine were radically overturned.

By a first rough count I came to the amazing total of thirty-one people who had answered the question on angels with a 'Yes'. That is 7.75% of the total survey.

If I go on to subdivide the experiences there appear to be great differences. A woman told me that she was very ill after a miscarriage. Then she suddenly had the feeling that she was picked up and as she lay there praying she heard beautiful music and a heavenly choir began to sing. Anyone who has heard something like that will never forget it. These angelic choirs are well known throughout history and I am of the opinion that Bach comes close to them in his two great Passions.

A nurse came to a great spiritual crisis. She worked on the night shift, but could not go on because of her sorrow and loneliness. And then, in the stillness of the night, she clearly felt a hand on her shoulder and a great sensation of comfort came over her.

This comforting, warming hand came up quite often in my stories. A rationalist shrugs his shoulders. Come, come, that can be explained completely in psychological terms. If that is supposed to be an angelic experience, we need not get excited.

For the rationalist, therefore, I have something more substantial. The Germans invaded Holland in long convoys of trucks. In Limburg a nice young girl was riding a bicycle; a truck passed her, and the soldiers began to whistle and wave. Furiously she turned her head the other way. The next truck swerved from its course, the driver trying to run over the haughty girl at full speed. Then, just before the truck hit her, she and her bicycle were picked up and put down several yards to one side, and the truck rushed by. A cyclist following the girl some twenty yards behind saw it all happen. He rode up to her and asked in amazement how he could have seen what he simply could not possibly have seen. The whole event was engraved on her memory, right down to the dress she was wearing.

A similar story was told to me by a man who was unable to get out of the path of a car speeding towards him, when he was carefully removed from his bicycle and deposited on the verge. The bicycle was totally crushed a second later, but the man was uninjured.

Angelic choirs, comforting hands, miraculous rescues.

A young man and a young women knew each other through the secret service. 'Right!' I can hear the reader think, 'Here comes some sort of James Bond story.' But in real life it is not like it is in the pictures. The secret service is often a hard and cynical business which makes heads empty and hearts cold. The hero and the heroine of this story had become, despite their comparative youth, people without illusions. They knew each other well but harboured a deep and real hatred for each other. I am not permitted to tell how and for whom they worked, only that the story took place in the Eastern Bloc; that he was Dutch and that she came from behind the Iron Curtain.

One day they had both reached a low point in their emotional life. An overruling despair had overtaken their lives. And then, after an official meeting which they both had to attend, something happened. They stood on the street and both were driven by an overpowering feeling towards a large cathedral, in an east European city. In the cathedral both of them felt a powerful hand which took them by the neck and forced them to surrender. The story has a happy ending: they are now married and live in Holland. From both of them emanates radiance, like people who have seen Hell and have realised that the light is always stronger.

There are just a few examples. The stories were stirring and the way they were told indicated that they had been very important to their storytellers. One could tell by the tone of the story how profound the experience had been. Very deep layers of consciousness had been touched. These were not experiences which flashed on and off along the surface of their existence, as happens with so many daily events. They touched the whole person. As the story was told, the voice lowered in pitch and the eyes looked inwards.

It was tempting to include all the people in this category of positive reactions in my survey. I did not do so because my question had been literally, 'Have you ever seen an angel?'

And then it appeared that this question too could be answered in the affirmative by a number of people, but that even amongst those who had seen them there were great differences. Time and again people told me about a powerful light that came to help them in moments of deep need. Typical is the story of a woman in the midst of a serious marital crisis. She would spend the night awake and praying, crying, 'Lord, save me!' The next day she suddenly fell over backwards and saw a clear powerful light. Great peace and happiness flowed through her. The problems were not solved but from that moment on she could see them in perspective; she could deal with them. Sometimes more than one person sees that light. One woman told me that as a child she had been seriously ill, and people feared for her life, her mother sat by her bed. The girl then dreamed that she was dead and saw an intense white light. Her mother saw it too and was very upset.

Was that an angel? Bible stories recognize the Shekhina, the great cloud of light often called the Divine Indwelling. Is that angel or God? Whichever it is, it is an experience that touches people to the very depth of their souls that is never forgotten and that brings happiness, comfort and frequently healing.

Still other people did see angels, but not while consciously aware — more in the way of visions.

A young woman developed a serious syndrome after the birth of her child. During the night she saw a silver ladder leading to heaven, and at the top of the ladder there stood an angel and she had to make an instant decision: Go on to the land of no pain or go back to her husband and child? She chose to go back and from that moment on she recovered.

A man lay in hospital, totally mangled after a car accident. Almost everything in him was broken — it was a case of sink or swim. Then he saw a porch through which light streamed; in it stood someone who beckoned. He wanted so much to enter that he pulled out his drip feed: only to reconsider his decision, and return to the here and now.

The ladder to Heaven as seen by Jacob in Bethel, and the Gate to Heaven, are still with us. It is only that this materialistic age has obscured them. And as I write this I notice that suddenly I am quoting Goethe: 'The world of spirit is not closed, your consciousness is closed, your heart is dead!'

But it is not only in altered states of consciousness that angels are seen. People can also sometimes see angels when fully conscious and again there are differences in what is experienced. Sometimes the experience is one of a powerful light. For instance, a man is sitting next to his fiancée in a church, when suddenly the place where the preacher stands is taken up by a powerful light. But it is not an intense light that hurts the eyes, it is of tremendous supernatural beauty. The preacher himself becomes invisible. My storyteller was so moved that the tears streamed from his eyes as he told me that story. The strange thing was that his fiancée had seen exactly the same thing.

Afterwards the couple asked the preacher if he had noticed anything, but he knew nothing about it.

The man told me that this experience was a precious secret in his marriage. He still remembers the supernatural peace emanating from the light.

This man, much later on, gave great support to oppressed Christians in several east European countries.

One of my best friends told me that he was standing next to a telephone when suddenly an angel walked in through the closed window. It had a nebulous, luminous appearance. This friend said to me: 'Now I understand why angels are shown with wings, it is their radiance.'

The angel said a few comforting words and then disappeared again. That was very important to him for at that moment he feared for his life.

Sometimes, and these instances I find perhaps the most mysterious ones, angels are seen as ordinary people.

One of my patients tells of how as a child she lived on a great country estate, and on the estate stood a farm. One day her mother heard from the doctor that the farmer's daughter was dying. Her mother went immediately to the farmer's wife to pray with her. Then, as they prayed, they heard the back door being rattled. The mother of my patient got up and looked, and there stood a youngish man. The man said, 'Woman, what is wrong?'

She answered, 'A child is about to die.'

The man walked straight to the child's bedroom, laid hands on her and cast out the illness in the Name of Jesus. Then he left through the back door and nobody ever saw him again. That was most curious in a country district where everyone sees all and knows everything about each other.

The child woke up out of her coma directly afterwards and was quite angry the next morning when she was not allowed to go to school. This happened some thirty years ago. The girl is still alive and now a grown woman.

I have heard more stories of this kind. The angel who appears in normal present-day clothing. He brought deliverance at times of need, and then disappeared in a direction which he could not possibly have taken. He was 'just gone'.

'What did those angels look like?' people often ask me.

In my stories they looked like young men with good, friendly and sometimes noticeably beautiful faces. But their outer appearance was so unimportant compared to the message or deliverance that they gave, that my storytellers really only talked about the message or the way they were saved. If I wanted to know what they looked like I had to ask especially.

Oddly enough, a few women who had heard about my angel research asked me rather sharply whether, 'they were always male'. I assured the ladies that feminism has not reached Heaven. There, masculinity has the connotation of 'permeated by the Spirit', femininity 'filled with feeling'. They do not put up with penis envy in Heaven.

I must now make a correction in my inventory. Some people told me that they had an angelic experience whereas according to me they had rather experienced the phenomenon of extra-sensory perception.

Such as the story of a man who remembered that before the war an Indonesian had taken him to a mountain and had then mumbled incantations for some time. A blue light surrounded the mountain and the Indonesian said that this was the angel of mid-Java whom he had summoned. The phenomenon took place in broad daylight and lasted about half-an-hour. The Indonesian had offered a sacrifice during the presence of the blue light.

This type of happening I would prefer to classify as parapsychological because we know that angels do not allow themselves to be called up or summoned. Angels and magic do not go together because magic is concerned with power whilst angels come from the sphere of love. In that land of love there is no knowledge of exercising power over others. Only of serving joyfully.

If I look at these doubtful cases, I see myself hesitating in seven instances. The persons said, 'That was an angel' and I say, 'That was parapsychology'.

From this you can see that assessment was not always easy. It seems as if there is a border country where you remain uncertain as to exactly what happened. I can therefore write down all the extraordinary experiences together as follows:

1.	Parapsychological experience	61 people
2.	Border line cases	7 people
3.	Angelic experience	31 people

Therefore I can add the seven people in category 2 to either group 1 or 3. Either thirty-one or thirty-eight people have had angelic experiences; 7.75% or 9.5% of those asked. Somewhere between these lies the actual number. When my survey had been completed it became known what kind of strange question I had put to people during surgery hours, and people began to turn to ask me questions:

1. Did the meeting with an angel happen in special circumstances?
2. Did it only happen to religious people?

Well now, starting with the thirty-eight people, that is including all the people in that group in the widest sense, it would appear that sixteen of these were in serious danger of their life and twelve were going through a profound spiritual crisis as a result of sorrow. Adding these groups together we see that twenty-eight of the thirty-eight people, that is about three-quarters, were in a critical state when they had their encounter.

As regards the second question: Of those thirty-eight people, seventeen appeared not to belong to any recognized remaining twenty-one, nine were Roman the rest belonged to various Protestant ng religious did not automatically appear to imply ve rights with regard to angelic visitations. I hope that I do not shock religious leaders with this statement. Even outside the recognized church there appears to be a hot-line to Heaven.

I should like to add here that anyone who has had such a radical experience can no longer disbelieve, from that moment on and for the rest of his life.

It is also important to examine the distribution of the sexes very closely. Of the thirty-eight people there were fourteen men and twenty-four women. This would appear to indicate a preference for members of the female sex on the part of the heavenly messengers. However, this is not so. Of the 400 questioned, 287 were women as against 113 men. If one considers that I began the survey on a random day and then consistently asked everyone the two questions till I reached the 400th patient, then one can see that there were simply more women during surgery hours. It is a well-known fact that women visit the doctor more often than men. The smaller number of men with angelic experiences appears therefore to be amply compensated from a mathematical point of view, by the smaller number of men in the survey. You could even speak of a slight bias in favour of men. In fact, angels do not seem to follow the modern Equal Opportunites Act but tend to adhere to the old biblical pattern in which it is quite possible to find a certain male bias as far as contacts with Heaven are concerned. It has yet to be discovered if this applies to a larger group of people. I doubt this as I gained the impression in the course of many conversations that in this twentieth century of ours it is the women who pass on the torch of belief.

But now I am going to play my own 'devil's advocate'. I am going to set drastic limitations to those thirty-eight cases.

The seven doubtful cases are taken out at once. That leaves me with thirty-one. And now, of those thirty-one, I am going to count only those cases as positive, where the person concerned is fully conscious (i.e. not in a coma or drowning or experiencing a vision) and perceives with his eyes (i.e. not just hearing or feeling) a complete angel (i.e. not just a pair of hands). That angel must also meet the condition that he had a clearly human shape and was thus not 'just' seen as a large white light bringing happiness and help.

By weeding my angelic garden that strenuously (with excuses to all those who met angels in some other way), six witnesses appear to be left who meet these rigorous conditions, 1.5% of the total questioned.

Let me give just one case: A deeply devout girl of twelve lived in menacing surroundings with people heavily involved in spiritualism. She often lived in fear and prayed fervently for help. One day while walking down a long, straight forest road a man suddenly stood in front of her. There was nowhere he could possibly have come from, and yet there he stood. He looked like a perfectly ordinary person, and he told her that she did not have to be afraid any more, and immediately she stopped being afraid once and for all. He also told her that her path would not be simple but that the Lord would always be with her.

This event left her feeling happy for a number of weeks and moreover from that moment she was able to differentiate between real and false spiritualism, that which is called in the New Testament the 'discernment of spirits'.

If we look at who those six people are then it would appear that they are very matter-of-fact people. One of them is the assistant manager of a large, partially nationalized company, another an industrial medical officer, one a hard-working housewife with several children, then comes the owner of a stationery store, a civil servant and another housewife.

Should I thus conclude from this survey that angels do really exist? Van Praag says somewhere that if, in the history of the world, just one man had demonstrated the phenomenon of levitation, and that after this no other person had encounted such a phenomenon, then nonetheless this would have demonstrated that levitation exists.

Consequently, my first conclusion arising from this research is that angels do exist. They are clearly part of the world of human experience.

If I now look again at the whole group (of thirty-eight) who had angelic experiences, then some things become quite noticeable. In the first place, a great feeling of blissfulness, and a strengthening, or confirmation of belief and the inner peace that emanated from the meeting. These feelings often lasted several weeks and could be vividly remembered many years later.

Whether an angelic experience is authentic can be tested through these emotions. An encounter with an angel is not simply a gruff acknowledgement somewhere along the street. It stirs a person to the depths of their being. The feeling that results has been inimitably recorded by Selma Lagerlof in 'Nils Holgersson' in the episode of the great Crane Dance on the Kullaberg:

'All who had come for the first time to the Kullaberg understood why the meeting as a whole was called after the Crane Dance. It contained savagery, but the feeling generated was yet more a sweet longing. Nobody thought about combat any more. On the contrary, all, those with wings and those without, wanted to raise themselves, glide above the clouds, search to see what lay behind, shake off that heavy body that pulled them down to earth and finally float away to the heavens.'

Probably the second point that needs mentioning is closely tied to the first one. All those persons who experienced such an event appeared to have kept the memory deep within themselves. It was often the first time they had ever told anyone about it. I met one couple where the husband answered my question with a laugh and said, 'No doctor, is that possible?' But the wife looked at the floor in an embarrassed way and then said hesitantly, 'I've never mentioned it before, John, but . . .' Very often the fear of being thought mad was given as the reason for this silence. Angels belong so little to the spirit of our hard materialist century that seeing an angel taints one immediately with madness in the eyes of the general public.

Yet I also believe that the depth of the emotions thus called forth tends to lead to the experience being hidden. Some experiences are simply too powerful to be put in words. This hesitancy to talk about angelic experiences is in complete contrast to supernatural observations. Perhaps I should say other supernatural observations, since catching sight of an angel is obviously not a normal event. Here I use the word supernatural for clairvoyance, clairaudience etc.

These phenomena are very much in fashion and people talk about them glibly and easily. One lady answered my question as to whether she had ever seen an angel with a radiant face, 'Oh no, doctor, but I do believe in gnomes!' Ever since the appearance of the popular book by Rien Poortvliet this seems permitted.

Nonetheless, angelic stories are sometimes told in intimate circles, such as this story that came spontaneously in answer to my question. The grandmother of one of my patients had told it to her.

Her father, that is the great-grandfather of my patient, had worked as a preacher in Africa. One day he had to use a lonely road in order to visit one of his parishioners, and along the road two bandits were lying in wait behind some rocks. The attack on the preacher did not take place because two men clad in white were seen to walk with him. The two robbers told this later on in the inn when they tried to find out who had protected the preacher. The innkeeper promptly

32

told this to the preacher when he went to warn him to be especially careful, but the preacher had not seen the protectors who had saved his life.

Again this is a typical angel story. More of this type of story is known in the missionary world but I chose this story because I heard it personally. Naturally, I have not included it in my statistics.

Actually we do not have to travel that far. Around the turn of the century there lived in a working-class part of Den Helder a baker, known as 'Blessed Breet'. On Saturday evenings the shop was cleared, chairs were set out and on Sunday morning he held a meeting for the people in the neighbourhood who were not members of a church. It was always full to bursting. He also ran a Sunday School at the bakers shop, and his Christmas celebrations were famous.

At that time Den Helder still retained a red-light district that was left over from the days when sea-going ships from Amsterdam passed through. The inhabitants of the red-light district were not especially happy about Breet's missionary work, since because of him several prostitutes had already left that life, and this was costing the gentlemen money.

Breet was also a faithful visitor of the sick, to be relied on by day and night. So one night it happened that he was woken from his sleep, and he poked his head out of the window and saw a man standing below.

'Mr. Breet', said the man, 'there's someone seriously ill at 24 Jansenstraat and they have asked for you.'

'I'm coming,' said Breet, dressing himself and going downstairs. The man had meanwhile disappeared.

In order to arrive at the given address he had to cross a narrow bridge over the canal. He rang the bell at no. 24. At first all was quite. However, after he had rung for a second time an angry voice behind the door asked what he wanted.

Breet said that he had been asked to come because someone was seriously ill.

'There is no sick person here and I don't need anyone,' said the angry voice. Disappointed, Breet went back home.

Twenty years later a man came into his shop. Breet stood behind the counter.

'Mr. Breet, I would like to speak to you', said the man.

'Come inside,' said Breet.

Then the man said: 'Do you remember that night about twenty years ago when you received a request to go to a sick person in the Jansenstraat?'

'Yes,' said Breet, 'I remember, that was not an experience quickly forgotten.'

'I was the man who came for you,' said his visitor. 'I hated you so much that I had agreed with a friend to drown you. We lured you to an address on the other side of the bridge and we waited at the bridge so we could throw you into the water. But when the three of you came we hadn't enough courage. At each side of you there was a companion.'

'No,' said Breet, 'I was on my own the whole way.'

'My friend and I clearly saw someone on each side of you.'

'Then the Lord must have sent angels to keep me safe,' said Breet with deep gratitude.

The visitor said that through his reading the New Testament he had been converted and now felt the need to confess all.

Breet's bakery nowadays serves as a mission hall and Sunday school, and the storyteller, Mr. J. Bijlsma, had, himself, conducted Sunday school in the building.

I have spoken to him. He did not know Breet personally but he had talked with a member of Breet's family who had told him the story. Moreover he had read the story in a book written by Breet about his life.

Back to my survey.

When I began the survey I had thought my conclusion would be: 'Angels were sometimes seen in the past, but not nowadays.'

With the survey behind me the conclusion must be: 'Angels are seen just as often as they used to be, but nobody talks about them anymore.'

If my group of 400 people is at all representative of a cross-section of the population, then we would be allowed to assume that at least 1% of the Dutch population has been face-to-face with an angel at least once in their life. That would mean that, assuming some fifteen million people, about 150,000 encounters with angels have taken place amongst the present population. That is an amazingly high number. Apart from which it would have to be one of the best-kept secrets of the century. It is almost unbelievable that this is possible given our talkative population. Even during the war, when lives were at stake, it was almost impossible to keep underground work a total secret, simply because we are so talkative.

I do not believe this number is accurate, since we forget one very important factor at the arithmetical stage, namely the man doing the research. I suspect that because of my attitude I attract far more people who have seen angels than someone making such a survey who feels it is a folly before even starting. In some mysterious way you seem to attract those things for which you feel an affinity. And more precisely it is those phenomena from the secret world which have a special inclination to pile themselves up against the person fond of that secret.

Let us take the extreme case that 99% of this collection of stories is due to me and the real number of angelic encounters is a mere 1% of what I found. This number of 1% is chosen completely at random but I wish to be on the conservative side.

If I can thus assume that the real proportion of angelic meetings taking place in the Dutch population is only 1% of what I found in the course of my survey, even then there must be some 1,500 Dutch people who have been face-to-face with an angel.

Fully conscious. And take note that it is 1,500 who have met the strictest limitations of the survey: complete visibility, full consciousness, human form.

That is quite a number — the secret association of angel spotters who have kept their secret well.

Perhaps there are pious people who are a little shocked at the way I have discussed my research. I am fully aware of my business-like manner.

When my research had only just begun, I asked a businessman if he had ever seen an angel. 'No', he answered, 'Has anyone ever seen an angel?' I had just 'caught' my first angel and had not yet interviewed my first hundred subjects. I told him this. 'Keep going,' he advised. 'In market research we speak of a response when we reach 2%.' I felt just like someone who wanted to set up an angel trading corporation.

And yet the man touched on something which is very important. The cool eye with which a possible market is analysed is one of the few methods which still possess the power of conviction in this century.

Even if you want to mislead the public in this second half of the twentieth century, you have to do so scientifically, using statistics, graphs and laboratory data. Only then do you stand a good chance of being believed.

Fortunately there is no easy fortune to be earned by this research into angels, so that you can be reasonably confident I speak only the truth in this chapter. If a fortune could have been earned, you can be fairly certain that someone somewhere would already have undertaken the research long ago — only they would have made use of an official authority, with subsidies and grants.

Angels appear to exist, even according to twentieth century standards. And that is an important fact. With that a clear light is thrown on the angelic stories throughout the centuries. Angels appear to all people and in all centuries.

They are not mythological additions by Eastern writers, as some people would have you believe. They do not belong in the same category as unicorns and trolls taken from fairy tales. They are facts which belong to life, which is why the Gospels describe them in the same matter-of-fact way as they do tax inspectors, soldiers and scholars.

There exists an art movement called magic realism. Here are depicted the bizarre and the impossible, painted in great detail and with natural forms. A woman has a right arm composed of an incredible ivy branch. Both woman and branch are depicted with loving faithfulness to nature, but the combination is of course impossible. Hieronymus Bosch was perhaps the first magical realist with his monsters that were made up from existing natural forms combined together.

I would like to plead now for the preservation of religious realism. An attitude that allows for the possibility that what is considered impossible and the reality of every day, can appear simultaneously. An attitude which allows for the possibility of an angelic encounter just as easily as the possibility of an old friend ringing at the front door. Perhaps that could inject some warmth into the growing businesslike attitude to relationships.

Naturally many people asked me, 'Have you yourself ever seen an angel?' Well, I feel immediately I ought to categorise myself, and with the deep contemplators at that. The answer would be, 'No, I've never seen an angel.' But I have had an experience which has allowed me to deepen my notions about angels, and for that I have to thank a perfectly ordinary whisp of cloud.

I have lived all my life in a part of Holland known as Kennemerland and I find that one of the most beautiful characteristics of this area is the endless variations of the sky. A man could spend a lifetime looking at the sky without ever getting tired of it. At one moment thunder clouds with a golden edge pile up at the horizon, and then appears a flock of pink fleecy clouds like sheep grazing at a high level. In the winter the snow showers drive past. One sees them as slashes of white paint set in contrast against the black sky in the west, whilst the sun lights them up from the east with its slanting rays. And in summer there are stately white clouds with fascinating transformations: an old man with a white goatee beard staring contemplatively at the horizon, a fat giant with a wrinkled forehead and a hooked nose threateningly opening his mouth in which hangs but one tooth from the upper jaw, an enormous snail with a towering shell on its back creeping out on the wings of the wind. And sometimes a strange light is cast and rain clatters down from a pitch black sky whilst all the time the sun cheerfully shines.

'The sun shines and it rains. It's all the fun of the fair in Hell', as my mother used to say. When you see that light: run quickly outside because then that black cloud curtain serves as a back drop for a rainbow, a phenomenon that each time leads to delight. What a price was paid for that rainbow! a whole civilisation was destroyed and a new world was born out of the water, in that long ago time of the Great Flood. And God, as a lasting reminder that something similar would never happen again, placed his bow in the clouds.

It was predicted that our world will not be destroyed by water but by fire. It looks as if we are doing our very best to make sure that this prophecy comes true as quickly as possible. What sign will God give to the heavens after our world has perished by fire? Will there be a green circle around the sun from time to time over the new world that will arise from the atomic ashes? As a sign that something like that will never be permitted again?

Nonetheless, the heaven of clouds and rainbows is not the heaven of angels. It is our sky, it is of the earth. Although you do have the feeling sometimes that it touches the heaven of the angels.

As a boy I lay one day in front of our house looking at the sky. The dahlias were in flower, the first spiders had spun their webs and I smelled that vague scent which told us: 'Autumn is coming!' A smell of wood fires, mixed with mushrooms, with a hint of something even more subtle that has no name. The air was mainly blue but the middle of the sky was taken up by a wisp of cloud at a very high altitude. And as I lay there looking at this cloud I saw that above the dunes soared a gigantic angel. The head shone from a surrounding soft cloth, draped as those worn by Arabs. The wings were partly spread and downy. The figure was wearing a long cloak hanging down to its feet but the feet themselves were invisible. The angel hung there without any movement, calmly regarding the countryside. The sky around seemed wider and deeper than usual. Sometimes a blue sky can feel like the tight glass bell cover to a cheese board starting immediately above your upward-looking eyes. But this blue was as wide as an ocean and bright as when the sun shines on the wavelets. Then the image was slowly blown apart and became again a cirrus cloud and the stillness of autumn lay over the countryside.

What do you really see at such a moment? Is your imagination projecting the image of an angel onto a cloud? Is a chance wind changing a high level mist into the image of a heavenly figure? Or is it something else?

In physics we know nowadays of a whole family of electrically charged particles. These travel through space at enormous speed. People have built what are known as cloud chambers in order to make them visible. In these you can record the track these passing particles leave using a photographic plate. You see a trail of droplets rather like the trail left by high-flying aircraft. Is it possible that an angel could momentarily leave a similar trail; that the invisible becomes momentarily visible when circumstances are favourable, or the imprint of the incredible is made onto the mists of this earth of ours?

In Africa I once climbed a mountain and there, clearly impressed on the flat rock, stood the gigantic tracks of some prehistoric reptile. An imprint of terrifying form, much more real than the surrealistic illustrations in books on the early history of our planet. It was almost as if the beast were gone for but a moment, and despite myself I searched the mountain slopes, expecting the gigantic head to reappear at any moment, looking at me hungrily from a cave.

Here the impossible had really existed and imprinted its existence on the soft wax of visible creation. Still, it was a prehistoric beast, just as corporeal as ourselves, if we are to judge by its size.

Could the really invisible occasionally leave its tracks on this world of ours? Putting the question in this way is to answer it: All that is real is invisible but appears here briefly in what is called a corporeal form only to disappear and become invisible once again. We are forcibly reminded of this each spring when the bare branches of the cherry tree bring forth thousands of delicate blossoms. That is a direct message from a higher or deeper world. That is also why in Hebrew the words for 'flesh' and 'message' are closely related. Everything that appears in the 'flesh', that is as matter, is a message from the other, secret world.

So I cannot really know whether or not I saw an angel. And yet, when I think of that autumn day, a great wide stillness surrounds me.

Actually it is really quite arrogant to be writing about angels. Even worse than Karl May[1] who managed to fascinate generations with his tales of Old Shatterhand and

1 Karl May, born in Germany in 1842 was an enormously popular writer of stories about Red Indians. He was widely read on the continent and held three generations spellbound with noble redskins, white rascals and of course a noble whiteskin by the name of Old Shatterhand, who happened to be a German. He befriended an equally noble Redskin, Winnetou.

Actually four years before his death Karl May visited the U.S.A. and stood eye to eye with real Red Indians, but this was after his books had been written.

Winnetou, even though he had never in his life been to America, still less seen a single Red Indian. But Karl May could have verified the existence of Red Indians by taking the boat to America. And there he would have found them, very much alive and quite real.

Someone writing about angels finds himself in a much more difficult position because there is nowhere specific he can travel to in order to test the authenticity of his stories. Or if he finally starts on the journey to the land of the angels, there is no way to come back and tell the tale. Nonetheless the whole ancient world was full of angel stories. Angels walked into people's homes, treated them almost familiarly, brought messages, in short they were part of the ancient pattern of things. There even appears to exist a sort of 'Angel Handbook' if I am permitted to express myself in this somewhat irreverent fashion.

I don't really know when this interest in angels started changing. Because at first there was a clear possibility that angels and people could encounter each other. After this there was more in the way of paintings and stories about angels. And finally angels were brought into the same category as the strange creatures in Grimm's stories and the Tales of Mother Goose. Although I think I can detect a very slight turn around in recent times.

However, in my youth angels were definitely not part of the possibilities of life. At least this was not so in our home, nor with most people I knew. You could, while walking in the dunes or the forest, come across a rabbit or a deer, but not an angel. They were not part of our consciousness. Do please realise this, because the story I am about to tell you made a deep impression on me, precisely because angels were the absent reality of my youth.

At our secondary school we had a Jewish geography teacher, a Mr Cohen. He often told us merely what seemed to us the dry facts of his subject but now and then he changed. The schoolmaster faded away and an old prophet appeared.

Neutral Norway was unexpectedly invaded by Nazi Germany on the 9th of April 1940. At the start of the lesson Mr Cohen walked to an alcove in the wall where the maps were hung on a rail. He then walked to the middle of the room with the map of Europe behind him. The class was silent. He took hold of his long pointer and indicated Germany and then Norway. Then he lifted up his two arms, holding the pointer in his right hand like the staff of a prophet, and said slowly, 'From today neutrality has ceased to exist in Europe.' That was a shocking statement, certainly in a country such as Holland, which more or less expected to remain neutral just as in the war from 1914 – 18.

Then, as if to prevent any further discussion, Mr Cohen said, 'We will now continue with the lesson.'

One month later Hitler's hordes invaded Holland and the words of Mr Cohen appeared to have been prophetic. Happily he survived the war. But now about that angel:

The invasion of Norway was not the first occasion when a prophet broke through the external appearance of a middle-aged Jewish schoolmaster.

On 30 November 1939 almighty Russia attacked tiny Finland. Holland collected skis for the Finnish soldiers but nobody really believed that the small Finnish army could really hold back the powerful red divisions.

Churchill writes in 'The Second World War' (Ch. XXX p. 426):

'The indignation excited in Britain, France and even more vehemently in the United States at the unprovoked attack by the enormous Soviet power upon a small, spirited and highly civilised nation, was soon followed by astonishment and relief.'

Finland was not trodden underfoot and everybody asked themselves how this was possible. Then one day Mr Cohen fetched the map of Scandinavia and showed us how the Russians attacked with a pincer movement and how the Finnish army escaped the pincer as if by a miracle. It was as if they had become invisible to the Russian invaders.

'It appears that something was seen,' said Mr Cohen at the end of his story and then went directly on to more mundane matters. Nobody asked him what he had meant by that last remarkable statement of his.

After the lesson was over I went up to him, together with another boy.

'What did you mean just now when you said that something was seen?' I asked. 'What was seen?'

Mr Cohen looked at us searchingly for a moment. Then he momentarily became 3000 years old instead of 50 and said, 'An angel, child'. 'Child' is what he called every boy.

We didn't dare ask any more and walked out of the classroom in bewilderment. Angels belonged to Christmas stories and nativity scenes. An angel in the middle of a modern war and a teacher that mentions this fact in the same way as he talks of the number of enemy divisions, why, that was an event with one more dimension than we knew, chilling and alarming.

It was here I personally discovered the fact that angels form an emotional problem in this century. You simply cannot react superficially. Now what could be the cause of this? I will cautiously try to give an explanation: Man can study a star with the aid of his great new telescopes or using space travel, and he can penetrate to the depths of the sub-atomic world with his electron microscopes — none of this chills him since it all relates to him. It is matter, so he can grasp it. Even if the star is far off or near, in a way it is in his power. Even if the radioactivity is formidable, he can control it from behind concrete or by using robots.

But here we are talking about a power which is beyond him. A power which cannot even in the long run be understood and controlled. No, a power which is as much above man as man is above one of his unfortunate laboratory animals.

It is that glimpse of the enormity that frightens people away. People do not want to hear about it out of pure fear, even if they try to hide this fear by dismissing the whole idea of superior beings with a supercilious smile.

We have lost something essential in this century, namely the respect for that which is above us. And if such an attitude makes itself master of humanity, then the higher powers sometimes break through in order to force us back to a little modesty. But back to Finland.

Much later I heard mention of the Finnish angel once again. Apparently, Russian divisions had surrounded a Finnish army unit. The Finns had prayed for help and in the middle of the night had seen a gigantic angel, hanging with outstretched wings above the Finnish camp. The Russians had not been able to find the surrounded Finns.

Perhaps this is merely a beautiful story, born out of the needs of those times. I have never spoken to a Finn who has seen an angel. But even if this is only a nice tale, it is still remarkable that even in the midst of our sober twentieth century stories about angels can circulate.

From this it appears that we can forget about angels but that they cannot forget us. They remain very much alive in human history and appear in times of need just as they used to.

Now you can easily find a way of explaining angels that would satisfy current ways of thinking. You simply say that angels are apparently anchored in the human framework as psychological facts. Facts which 'apparently' manifest themselves externally in times of need. As a projection from within, as you can see with small children. A child walks along a country path on a dark winter evening, and suddenly a silhouette of a fir seen against the night sky can change into a bogeyman watching as he lies in wait. Can you remember the intense relief when it appears to be a tree after all?

Psychoanalysis has even made God into a projection of a father figure. In any event it sounds extremely adult and scientific if you talk about 'the angel as psychological fact'. You are allowed to take part. Just imagine that a company of learned theologians has gathered and somebody holds a discourse on angels. He finishes his talk with the sentence, 'Whatever we may think about it, one can discuss the existence of angels as a psychological concept.'

The whole company would nod agreement. That is the uncommitted, scientifically balanced language which allows you to move in all directions. The language which may well have allowed you to loose your faith but which ensured your appointment as a professor.

And then a young preacher who has only just graduated stands up. I'm thinking of a particular type that can still be seen wandering around such as the well-known youth-work minister who managed to appear at his graduation in pajamas and explain to his professors, 'I stand here in my pajamas because the people at this university have not led us into belief but simply allowed us to go to sleep.'

That sort of a person.

And that man says, right there and then, in my imaginary theologians' gathering, 'Yesterday I met an angel.'

Can you imagine it? The irritation. The supercilious smiles. The shrugging of shoulders. And the unavoidable joker who stands up and with a fat grin asks, 'Was she pretty?' Then the laugh of relief of all those learned gentlemen. And the quick change of subject to serious matters such as the archetypal explanations of Jung and possibly the role of the angel in Mediaeval art.

No, angels are not welcome in the holy halls of science. Yet we must realise that science is very one-sided and therefore unable to pass judgement about matters which are real, but not open to scientific analysis.

This leads me to the following story:

The futurologist Willis Harman has recently rescued a fable from oblivion about a man who empties the whole ocean of fish using a trawl-net. The holes in the net were exactly one inch by one inch. When he examined his catch, which, as can be imagined, consisted of whales, dolphins, sharks, herrings, turtles, etc. etc., he wrote a thesis which gained him a doctorate in zoology. One of his propositions in that thesis was: Animals smaller than one inch in diameter are not found in the ocean.

For the same reason angelology, the study of angels, is not taught at universities any more. Angels are not found any more because the meshes of our net are too large. They slip away between the meshes of our patterns of thinking. And that is a great pity because in that way we have become just like people who have lost their shadow. And you may possibly know that this happened sometimes to people who sold their souls to the devil.

That is why I decided not only to set down the results of the angel survey but to couple it to a text book on angels. By way of gratitude to what those silent guides on our path do for us.

2. Guardian Angels

You might try noticing how often people who have been saved from a dangerous traffic situation make the following remark, 'That must have been my guardian angel!'

In our de-Christianised world the guardian angel lives on, just as though nobody has bothered to tell him that he does not belong there any more. Yes, it could even say that stories about guardian angels are on the increase.

There exists a nice American periodical which I recommend to everyone. It is called 'Guideposts' and regularly contains stories about angels. For instance in the issue of March 1982 a young woman called Euphie Eallonardo tells us:

'It had been reckless of me, taking a before-dawn stroll through the tangle of streets behind the Los Angeles bus terminal. But I was a young woman arriving in the great city for the first time. My job interview was five hours away, and I couldn't wait to explore.

Now I'd lost my way in a Skid Row neighbourhood. Hearing a car pass, I turned and, in the flash of light, saw three men lurking behind me, trying to keep out of sight in the shadows. Trembling with fright, I did what I always do when in need of help. I bowed my head and asked God to rescue me.

But when I looked up, a fourth man was striding towards me in the dark. Dear God, I'm surrounded. I was so scared, it took me a few second to realise that even in the blackness I could see this man. He was dressed in an immaculate workshirt and denim pants, and carried a lunchbox. He was about 30, well over six feet. His face was stern but beautiful (the only word for it).

I ran up to him. "I'm lost and some men are following me," I said in desperation. "I took a walk from the bus depot — I'm so scared."

"Come, " he said. "I'll take you to safety."

He was strong and made me feel safe.

"I . . . I don't know what would have happened if you hadn't come along."

"I do." His voice was resonant, deep.

"I prayed for help just before you came."

A smile touched his mouth and eyes. We were nearing the depot. "You are safe now."

"Thank you — so much," I said fervently.

He nodded. "Good-bye, Euphie."

Going into the lobby, it hit me. Euphie! Had he really used my first name? I whirled, burst out onto the sidewalk. But he had vanished.'

This is the modern angel story. It's a typical example. It contains a number of frequently recurring and clearly differentiated elements.

In the first place the extremely dangerous situation. I myself have been to Los Angeles and even as a man it is not safe to walk alone in the dark in certain neighbourhoods. The woman really went in danger of her life.

In the second place the sudden rescue by a normally-dressed young man. Often they are described as 'noticeably beautiful' even though their appearance is not especially effeminate. The seriousness is also discernible.

And finally the sudden complete disappearance of the rescuer, after it became clear that he knew more about one than was reasonable.

An angel in jeans with a lunchbox. Surely that is profanement of the sacred? Where are the white clothes? Where are the wings?

Now it is certainly true that most of us have no difficulty in breaking away from the image of an angel as a small chubby child with a vague suggestion of a shawl about the loins and a couple of ineffective wings on the back. That is the way they appear on Italian frescoes and they were probably made to comfort the parents in those times of high child mortality.

As far as those fat children with wings are concerned: The daughter of one of the people I questioned said thoughtfully one evening to her mother: 'Mummy, those angels cannot fly, the wings can't support them!'

If a child dies, does it become an angel, as the Dutch poet Vondel thought? I don't know the answer, but an angel can definitely manifest itself as a child. Here follows the words of another of my interviewees, a nice and slightly older man with the typical lustre in his eyes that I am gradually learning to recognise as characteristic of those who have cast a glimpse 'behind the scenes'.

At the age of nine he always saw, just before going to sleep, someone who looked like a child of his own age. That was accompanied by a tremendous feeling of happiness. The child was blond and was enveloped in a sort of shining lustre. After this had occurred for a couple of weeks the child said: 'This can't go on any longer because now your feet are touching the ground.' Then he disappeared and the boy never saw him again.

That's why I believe that an angel, if necessary, can appear to a child in the form of a child in order not to scare the little person he is visiting. Just as God, the Creator of heaven and earth, visited humanity in the form of a man.

These incidents take place out of the love for those being visited. We must therefore be careful not to throw the baby out with the bathwater, otherwise before we know it we will be left with an empty heaven populated only by a few whirling astronauts.

And while I am talking about children I would like to continue with another story out of 'Guideposts' (April 1983). William T. Porter from Englewoods, Colorado, tells us:

'We were standing in my parents' front yard saying good-bye when we heard her scream — it was our little daughter, who was two-and-a-half years old. Rushing to the backyard, we found Helen standing in the centre of the flagstone sidewalk, crying and dripping wet. It was apparent that she had fallen into my parents' small but deep fish-pond. Thank God she was safe! Then, as my wife rushed over to pick Helen up, it hit me. I couldn't see any wet footprints anywhere around the pond, yet our baby was standing a good 20 feet away from the water. The only water was the puddle where she stood dripping. And there was no way a toddler could have climbed out of the pool by herself — it was six or seven feet in diameter and about four feet deep.

As Helen grew up, we often puzzled over those strange circumstances. She herself had no memory of the event; she was, however, haunted by an intense fear of water.

Many years later, when Helen and her soldier husband were living in San Antonio, she began to work through that fear with the help of an army chaplain, Pastor Claude Ingram. After spiritual counselling and prayer sessions, he asked her to go back in memory and relive the frightening fish-pond experience. She put herself in the scene again and began describing the pond and the fish in detail. She cried out as she relived the moment of falling into the water. Then suddenly Helen gasped. "Now I remember!" she said. "He grabbed me by the shoulders and lifted me out!"

"Who did!?" asked Pastor Ingram.

"Someone in white," she answered. "Someone pulled me out, then left." '

Here we see an angel dressed in white. According to pious people this is as it should be. Nonetheless we have always known that inhabitants of the other world can show themselves here as ordinary people.

That's why the angel in jeans with his lunchbox fits neatly into the old Jewish legend which tells that Elijah will appear in each age dressed in the clothing of that period, as farmer, as labourer, as old man. Only afterwards can one say: 'That could have been Elijah.' In these times he, or the angel from heaven, would quite easily have appeared dressed in jeans.

One of the first angelic stories I heard in my surgery was from a dear old lady. One day she said suddenly to me: 'Doctor, do you believe in angels?'

'I certainly do,' I said.

Then she told me the following story. It happened during the war. At the time she lived in Heemstede and her son was studying medicine in Amsterdam. One Sunday evening she brought her son to what was called the Blue Tram which in those days went all the way to Amsterdam.

Each time it still amazes me to discover what makes mothers anxious. The boy was half Jewish on his father's side; what's more the hated occupation forces were actively hunting down young men in order to force them into the German armament industry. And yet that was not what caused the mother to worry at that moment. What concerned her was that he was going to ride a bicycle carrying a microscope and she was scared that he was going to fall off it in Amsterdam. Often our conscious thoughts imagine a small disaster in order to keep a great disaster at bay.

The boy managed to calm her down by promising to be very careful and then got onto the tram. The mother was very relieved and skipped rather than walked as she crossed the rails on the other track in the wake of the departing tram.

At that moment two powerful hands gripped her from behind, by her elbows, and dragged her away from in front of the wheels of the tram rushing towards her from the opposite direction.

Her rescuer let go of her and she turned round wanting to

thank him, but there was no-one to be seen. She stood there totally alone.

She is still alive and she is in her nineties, her mind as clear as ever. She was intensely interested when she heard that her story was to be put down in writing once more.

'A pity that there were no witnesses,' perhaps some people will say. But then I would remind them that amongst my thirty-eight people there were two who were snatched away from the path of onrushing cars in front of another person.

'Then why do so many accidents happen?' asks the same inveterate critic. 'Don't these angels pay attention?'

Later on I hope to discuss this question more fully. First we must ask ourselves whether each person really has a personal guardian angel; an idea which is talked about with much greater frankness amongst Catholics than Protestants; If this is so, there must be a great many angels. The prophet Daniel tells us of 'ten thousand times ten thousand' who stand before the throne of God (Daniel 7, verse 10).

The Revelations of St John, which in many ways is a sequel to the book of Daniel, also talks about the many angels around the throne, of which the number is ten thousand times ten thousand (Revelation 5, verse 11). The arithmetic works out at one hundred million.

And Jesus, speaking about children, says that their angels do always behold the face of His Father which is in heaven (Matthew 18, verse 10). That also quickly gets us to quite a few hundred millions on this planet.

The fact that so few people see angels is apparently not then caused by their infrequent occurrence.

There is an old Jewish story which tells that each person is accompanied down the path of life by two angels. The one on his right hand inspires him to do good and records his good deeds, the one on the left hand side nudges him towards evil and records his evil deed. The Catholic Church has taken over this idea, only one does not use the term 'evil impulse' but speaks of the 'angel which leads us into temptation'.

If this story is true then twice as many angels are to be found on this earth as there are people, a disturbing thought. And then again there is the children's verse that goes: 'Four angels to my bed, Four angels round my head, One to watch and one to pray, And two to bear my soul away.' (Thomas Ady; A Candle in the Dark). Well, even as a child I felt that this was a little more than was strictly necessary.

In view of these vast hosts of angels let us ask the question: 'What is an angel really?' This question cannot be easily answered. Are they separate creations; or a completely different race; or were they ever human beings?

The difficulty is caused by the fact that they manifest themselves only in their saving and protecting functions, at least as far as guardian angels are concerned. Yet when people encounter angels they are usually so overcome by emotion that nobody ever asks: 'Who or what are you really, tell me something about yourself.'

Allow me to show what I mean with an example.

In 'Appointment in Jerusalem', Lydia Price describes how in 1929 she was trapped between warring Jews and Arabs. The hostilities were already in full swing even in those days. She found herself in an Arab house where the water supply had been cut off and she was looking after a Jewish child that was almost one year old that she had saved from starvation. To go out into the street meant certain death since the Arabs shot anything that moved. Very shortly she found herself facing the awful choice between staying in the house to die of thirst, or to go out into the street and be shot.

Trusting totally in the help of God she picked up the child and went out into the street. It was quite still, not a shot was fired. There were barricades everywhere and, after some time, she reached one which she could not get over while still holding the child, and in despair she sat down. Suddenly a young man about six feet tall, in European clothes stood in front of her, he appeared to have come from nowhere. Quietly he took the child from her and went before her over the barricade and through the streets of Jerusalem and still not a shot was fired.

The man stopped in silence in front of a house and passed the child back to her. When she looked properly she realised it was the house of an English girl friend who was totally astounded to see that she had come through it all in one piece. The young man who could not possibly have been there and who had brought her through a no-go area to a house which he could not have known about, had vanished. Now, I ask you to walk with Lydia on this journey. Thirsty, afraid, expecting a bullet at any moment. And then the unexpected help. The unreal silence after all that shooting. The man who walked in front of her with the child. Would you, in those circumstances, have said to that man, 'Excuse me sir, but I have a strong suspicion that you are an angel. And since I'm talking to you anyway, I would like to put a few interesting questions to you about the nature of angels. Do you mind if we have a little chat?' If you agree with me that this is absurd then I hope that I have made it clear why we cannot depend on eye-witnesses when it comes to learning more about the nature of angels.

We must go back to much older sources. Our twentieth century may be technologically speaking very clever, yet older civilisations knew much more about the hidden side of the creation and left messages about it. Our purely technological superiority over earlier centuries has made us arrogant and allowed us to come to totally the wrong conclusions concerning our forebears. We think that, because people in the Middle Ages had no cars, therefore, necessarily they also held wrong beliefs. That is why so many articles begin nowadays with: In days of old people thought . . . but nowadays we know . . . We take it in together with our first solid food. People used to think wrongly, but nowadays they know better.

But when it comes to knowledge about the 'other side' we are barbarians compared to our ancestors. That is why it is useful to integrate their ideas with our thoughts about angels. Well, the old sources tell us about a number of interesting matters.

In the first place we have inherited the word 'angel'. It comes from a Greek work: 'angelos', a messenger. The Hebrew word for angel, 'malach', means exactly the same: a messenger or an envoy. It is of course a messenger from another world, but basically we can call anybody who brings a message an angelos. Postmen are thus very nearly celestial. Now the angels, as we have seen already, come suddenly into this world. My teacher of biblical Hebrew tells me that this is the deeper symbolism of angel wings. Because the word that indicates 'wings' in Hebrew also means a 'corner'. In English we talk about the 'wings' of large buildings. The angel has a capacity that we lack, namely to be able to step bodily round the corner of our world, perform the task and then step back to the other world around this corner. We have retained this idea in the expression 'a turn for the worse' to refer to someone about to die. He departs for another world where we, trapped in this world of three spatial dimensions, cannot follow him. Somebody who read the manuscript of this book gave me a striking confirmation of this 'corner'. I let her speak for herself:

'I would like to tell you a little about an experience I had while having an operation on my gall bladder, under a general anaesthetic. I was suddenly surrounded by a golden light in an environment where all was good. And not just good, it was wonderful. I saw nothing and nobody, there was only this light, but I knew everyone was there, everyone I love and would like to be near.

After having spent some time (who can tell how long) in this light, there was suddenly a voice which said that I must go back. 'Oh no', I cried. I resisted strongly because I did not want to return to the world. I saw my life, and in fact all earthly life, as a laborious dark-grey mush — where we are sucked down as in quicksand — pass by in a flash and I wanted to stay where I was.

Nonetheless I had to go, and funnily enough I was told that I still had a task to perform. Funny, because I was not the sort of person who thought about life in that way, as if I had indeed a task to perform.

In any case, I went. And how did I go? Round the corner. Literally, whereas around me was nothing other than this golden radiant light, suddenly there was a dark corner which I turned and then it went lower and lower and even darker and finally I heard a voice which said: 'Mrs Jones, Mrs Jones'. It was the surgeon who was calling me. That is all but naturally I did not forget it. I needed almost a year to get used to feeling at home again here and join in with everything. I really wanted to go back to where I had been for that short while.'

My teacher told me another bit of Jewish tradition. And that is, that angels always stand with their feet together. This is symbolic of the fact that they do not know the duality of this life. The duality of man and woman, good and evil, light and darkness. They are, as reflections of God, completely unified. The old painters must have certainly felt this. When you look at the faces of angels it is often unclear whether you are seeing a man or a woman. And yet neither are they effeminate men nor butch ladies. They are otherworldly, where the difference just does not exist in this way.

The laws which remind us all day long that we are bound to matter obviously do not apply to angels.

Someone who can step out of this heavy world will have little difficulty in overcoming the law of gravity. Again a characteristic story from that same Guidepost magazine.

The writer is Lloyd B. Wilhide from Keymar, Maryland.

' "Ask and it shall be given you," Jesus said. I have always believed this, but never so totally as the day of the accident in 1978.

I was 75 years old. The grass on our 121-acre dairy farm needed cutting, so I hitched a set of mower blades to my tractor and went to work. The tractor was huge, and for added traction up our undulating Maryland terrain, its rear wheels were filled with 500 pounds of fluid, and a 200-pound weight hung from each hub.

When I finished the job, I was on a slight uphill gradient near our chicken house. I switched off the ignition and climbed down from the high seat. I was unfastening the mower blades when the tractor started moving backwards.

I tried to twist around and jump up onto the seat, but I did not make it. The tractor's draw-bar hit me in the knees, knocking me flat, and the 700-pound left wheel rolled over my chest and stopped on top of it. I struggled for breath. The pain was agonizing. I knew I was facing death, and I made my request.

"Please, God," I begged, "release me." At that moment the tractor began to move.

It went forward enough to free my chest, and — to my amazement — it moved uphill!

My dog, and then a farmhand, found me; though suffering six broken ribs and two fractures, after twelve days in hospital I was back home, talking with the Maryland state trooper called in to investigate the accident. "I won't try to explain it officially," he told me. "Why, a dozen men couldn't have moved that tractor off you."

Twelve men or 1200, it did not matter. Asking God's help did.'

But, you are bound to ask, where was the angel? Is this now an example of a guardian angel?

I would like to ask another question in return: If some force pushes a tractor whose motor is switched off uphill against a slope, is not that force being applied by 'someone'?

Here we immediately get into all sorts of difficulty. In our first class at elementary school we all learned that $1 + 1 = 2$. The teacher did not tell us what that was all about. They were just numbers which you added and did not refer to chickens, apples or marbles. That was our first baptism in abstract thinking and it dried up something in us.

Then, when we grew a little older we learned that one gallon of water weighed some nine pounds. But the teacher did not tell us what that word 'weighed' meant.

That gallon of water was pulled to the earth or was it perhaps pushed? The force of gravity was actually hidden in that word 'weighed' and we did not think any further about it.

We grew yet older and we learned that electricity flowed through a wire. But nobody could tell you exactly what was that mighty force which made electric trains run and lit up houses.

Making use of forces that we do not understand becomes so natural that we forget to ask ourselves: what is it, a number, a weight, a force?

That is why we look on helplessly when suddenly, as in the story above, a force starts working intelligently. But could not electricity and gravity always be forces that have something to do with an intelligent 'conceptualizer' behind it all? And is it not therefore quite normal when we suddenly see that force abandon its normal rôle for a moment and lend a helping hand? If we imagine that in reality electricity and gravity are extensions of the arms of the Creator but disguised in such a way that everyone thinks they are dealing

with unthinking forces, then are we not dealing in the above case with a momentary dropping of the mask? A tiny instant of compassion on the part of a power which we think of as a blind force? And is that not an angel? Because it is said that an angel is an act of God. If God acts we immediately see an angel, and God is not blind force. He is such an individual, through and through, that when He acts it is not blind energy which is developed, but a creature that carries out His will.

Hume states as one of his propositions that in the case of a miracle one must always choose the least unlikely. Well, the least unlikely is that a guardian angel gave the tractor a little push so that he abolished the force of gravity for an instant. All other explanations are much more difficult and contrived. From the name 'messenger' we can deduce that even this type of wonderful event, where not a word is said, has a purpose other than being delivered from certain death. That old farmer of 75, for instance, will die in any case within the foreseeable future from some cause or another. There will always be amongst us the type of know-all who remarks disparagingly that it seems strange that from a statistic point of view, at the very moment that the old farmer was saved several children with their whole lives before them were killed in accidents.

Would it not have been better to have saved them? No, that is not how it works. The rescue is primarily a message and it reads: There is a heaven. That heaven is not far from us but nearby. Contact with heaven is possible and deliverance can come from there. There is a Creator who is personally involved with his creatures. And perhaps this old farmer was exactly the type of man who could transfer this message.

If forces like electricity, gravity, magnetism, wind, tides and sunlight are only the material manifestations of a hidden and conscious thinking, why do we not perceive any of this? I believe, and I will be coming back to that later on in the book, that this force is deliberately hidden from us.

If we felt the south wind as the breath of the angel Michael or the force of gravity as the power of another angelic hierarchy, then we would have remained dependent children, overwhelmed by the grandeur of our elders.

But in our intellectual development we have decided to give those conscious forces abstract names. We make those forces subservient to our needs and the forces allow this with great long-suffering.

We are as savages listening to a radio broadcast. We hear the voice in the little box but do not comprehend that somewhere a real man is talking.

Now the real question forces itself on us: Is man really so important that all sorts of angels have to involve themselves with him? Take a look at this galaxy in which we live. A disc-like clump of millions of stars, many of them much bigger than our sun. That galaxy itself is only one out of many millions, and not even one of the big ones.

Around that little sun of ours, known as a 'white dwarf' in astronomical terms, revolve small planets as tiny dust particles in the cosmos. And an almost vanishingly small item on that planet is a semi-malignant grasshopper: man. Would Heaven really be concerned? If you insist on believing something strange is it not much more likely that highly developed astronauts landed on this planet some time in the distant past? And that they have formed the existing humanity by constant manipulation? And that now and then they come to take a look at how everything is getting along in their colony? I am merely referring to a currently popular theory. In fact, however droll this theory may seem, it is a materialistic caricature of the ancient idea that man has descended to earth, has been planted on this earth. And by heaven it is not meant some distant planet in another galaxy. Since that would still be the same material world.

No, a deeper, finer, qualitatively different realm is meant. A land of which our material world is only a passing shadow.

And then man certainly becomes, despite his small stature, quite important. You can then imagine that the inhabitants of heaven watch him anxiously while he walks round on the earth, just as we watch the moon walkers with great interest on our television screens.

Now it is difficult to describe heaven, that other world, in everyday words. Ordinary words do not adequately describe it. That is why people from ancient times onwards have talked about heaven and its connection with earth in terms of parables. Usually the ordinary moral falls wide of the mark but at least you invite people to think about these things.

I shall therefore try to describe what guardian angels are really doing by means of an analogy. Keep in mind that I will be making mistakes because I am trying to describe a world of more dimensions seen from a world of fewer dimensions. I am trying to describe a three-dimensional sphere from within a two-dimensional circle. Anything is better than nothing, so here goes.

Every Dutchman knows that on the Terschelling coast lies a legendary treasure. And that all the time people are setting up salvage parties who set to work with all sorts of apparatus for a few months, only to finish up triumphantly with a single piece of gold — probably thrown in by the captain to 'seed' the proceedings — and that divers go down to bring up the rest of the treasure after which nothing more is ever heard. You will probably have noticed that a lot of equipment is necessary in order that a diver can work in deep water. A ship is needed on the surface from which the whole operation can be supervised. The divers have to wear diving suits, they need air lines to the ship or aqualungs, telephone cables or walkie-talkies. And there is also usually a cable on which they can tug when they want to be pulled up out of the water.

Well, that is more or less the position of we mortals on this earth. We have been dropped down into time for some period and we are all searching for treasure. We have even received detailed instructions of the kind of treasure we should be collecting that it is to be of the type that can be taken back up. And probably we are pulled up every night so as to take a breather, and that at our death we are pulled up permanently.

You did not really think we could do all this without some help, here at the bottom of the well of time. Do you not think there is a continual celestial back-up team ready to help us with our supplies and feedback?

Perhaps you would prefer another analogy to our journey on this sublunar world. Think of man's journeys to the moon. How an enormous staff is necessary at Houston in order to deliver two men there. If you then compare this to our own position then the children's rhyme about the four angels (or if you read it slightly differently and add them all together, the twelve angels) is not quite so preposterous. The celestial Houston has possibly to retain a large staff to make our existence possible.

Up to now in this chapter I have been talking about sudden situations that became so dangerous for us down here that somebody from 'ground personnel' was required to rush up to us in order to help. But is that really the normal situation? The situation in which we usually find ourselves? Fortunately we do not continually find ourselves at death's door.

According to the analogy there would have to be crew available to make our stay possible. Apparently we, on this planet, have something important to do since so much help is necessary. That something important has been given several names. Metanoia is one of them: an altering of consciousness. Continual help is necessary for our work and this flows continually towards us. How is it then possible that most of us are not aware of this background?

Let us take the analogy of the divers a little further. The diver (or the moon-walker, who is in many ways similar to a diver) had two vital needs: oxygen and information.

Then take our own position on earth. We also have two constant needs. In the first place we must be provided with life, or else our body immediately becomes a corpse. Let no one think that he makes his own heart beat or that he has any control over the complicated metabolism of his cells. These processes are unconscious and are controlled from the 'surface ship' or the 'celestial Houston'. While we sleep many parts of our body are repaired, but this is not done 'automatically'! No, conscious and intelligent beings are at work, just as conscious and intelligent beings put 'a man on the moon'. Here we are dealing with the same thing in reverse. Heaven has placed a man (or a woman) on this earth. And as earth is a complicated sort of place to live on, care of the body has to be perfect, otherwise we will not last out and will in fact die.

It is a pity that this gift, which is conveyed to us each day anew, is accepted in such a careless way. Yes, we have become so estranged from what is really happening that we demand that our doctor repairs our faulty health as quickly as possible whenever something goes wrong with our body. As if at a garage we demand: 'I need the car again next week, will it be ready on time?'

Just as interesting as the bodily needs is the need for information. If we have guardian angels, leaving aside for a moment the exact nature of these creatures, then what do we notice of them in the course of our daily lives? It would really be quite remarkable if those intelligent creatures were to be intensely involved with us, yes even to the extent of helping us directly, without us noticing anything.

Let us concentrate for a moment on our ordinary everyday life.

Do you drive a car? If so, do you know that strange feeling of 'I think I will just go carefully past that alley' . . . and just then a cyclist zooms out in front of your car. Or 'I think I will keep to the near side on that bend' and along comes a heavy truck and trailer on your half of the road. Is that radar? Come off it, surely we are not bats. Or are we? Well, whose radar then? Is it not much more likely that we were given a warning sign from celestial control? Is it not rather arrogant to think that this is just our intuition?

Another example. I once had a patient, a friendly girl with an acute anxiety complex. She had been lying in bed already for several days, shivering with fear and not daring to move even a single step. Drug therapy for anxiety was then in its very early stages. Although she was dead set against it, I was on the point of having her taken into psychiatric care.

With this problem occupying my mind I fell asleep one evening. The next morning I woke up and just on the border-line between being asleep and being awake I saw a small light-brown rabbit with a white nose hopping over my bed.

At eight o'clock my assistant arrived and I said, 'Somewhere in this neighbourhood there is a small light-brown rabbit with a white nose. Would you be so good as to fetch it?'

Without asking for an explanation, my assistant took the car and came back an hour later with exactly the rabbit I had seen hopping over my bed. She never told me where she found it. I put the animal into my Gladstone bag and went to the frightened patient. With a face distorted by fear she lay there looking at me.

'I have something for you,' I said, and opened the case. I lifted the rabbit onto her bed, and immediately it started hopping over her blanket. A look of great tenderness came over her face and from that moment her fear left her.

'Clever thinking', someone will remark. Not at all, a thing like that is not my doing. I could not possibly have thought of something like that. Surely it is much more probable that my angel made contact with her angel and said, 'What exactly is the problem?' And that her angel said, 'Give her

66

something to cherish, something that is even more afraid and more vulnerable than she herself.' And that my angel looked around, saw the rabbit, passed the image on to me and that the angel of my assistant informed her where to find the animal. Such a supposition only requires three angels. And although I do not know whether the conversation between the angels took exactly that form, I do know that they speak in tongues. St Paul says so, and he should know.

All other ways of explaining this case are more complicated. I am of the opinion that the solution using three angels is the simplest, the most elegant and therefore probably the right one. That which we like to call 'coincidence' and which comes dropping from heaven, becomes much more comprehensible when we assume that in reality we are dealing with a case of being constantly watched over by intelligent beings.

These beings are characteristically very modest, and they permit us to think that all these coincidences and intuitions are due to our own superiority.

A few examples: Early one morning I was walking along the promenade in Tijuana, Mexico. The ocean came into the bay in long rolling waves. It was incredibly beautiful to see, and I wanted to stand at the edge of the promenande and watch. But something was holding me back from taking even a single step. I walked a little further to one side and from my new position I could see that the sea had washed the ground from under the promenade for several yards. The concrete slab, some several yards square, that had appeared to be a stable part of the road was really a sort of trapdoor that was barely connected at only one side to the rest of the road. It virtually hung in the air and the beach lay about twelve feet below. Further along several large concrete slabs had apparently already fallen down. The step I had not taken had saved me, since if I had taken it that might have been the straw that broke the camel's back and if you were to land underneath such a capsizing slab the chances that you would survive in one piece were not great. Was that instinct? Most unlikely, I have evolved far too much away from nature. A quick signal from a celestial radar station? I think that is what I will stick to.

Let us take another example. Opposite me sits a couple having a difficult conversation. He looks apologetic, she is full of irritated aggression. She is obviously very suspicious of me and is annoying me a lot. 'That man does not have an easy time with a woman like that,' I think. And suddenly something happens inside me. For an instant I see that woman as a child. A loving hopeful child. Then I see her as a young woman.

Nice, radiant, enjoying the prospect of a happy marriage. And then all sorts of things go wrong, disillusion follows disillusion and life goes sour. And I say, 'Do you know that despite being so difficult just now you really are a very nice woman'. And then suddenly the woman starts to cry and she sobs, 'Nobody has said anything like that to me for years.'

Now I want you to notice something. I myself was irritated, was totally inclined to sympathise with the husband. Who showed me that picture? It certainly did not come from me. I am not that nice inside. That was surely sent to me. Because if two people start to interact two angels at the command centre start looking too. And if you give them half a chance they will intervene. Because, although I used the words command centre just now, it is just there that the hold-up takes place.

We all switch off this communicating link with the celestial monitoring centre during large parts of the day. Or perhaps it is not so much that we switch it off as that there is too much interference, so that we cannot receive the broadcasts.

Three times during my life my car has been totally wrecked by a truck through no fault of my own, and I remember that on each of those three occasions such emotional storms were raging inside me that I could not possibly have picked up any warning.

Why are those vitally important voices so soft? Why did God's voice reach Elijah neither in the midst of the storm, nor during the earthquake, nor by fire (a volcanic eruption?), but came as — so the Hebrew text says literally — 'a still small voice'? (1 Kings 19, verse 12).

Because one of the most important tasks on this planet is that we must freely develop ourselves and that again is necessary because only someone who is free can love. Forced love changes into hate. Love for God and our neighbour, which is what all this is about, is only possible in a free environment. And we would not be free in the eyes of heaven if at any moment we were overwhelmed by messages. That is why it has to be an event of tremendous suffering when someone is called to be a prophet. That is also why so many prophecies begin with the expression, 'the burden of . . .' A prophet is a beast of burden. He lifts his prophecy up with difficulty and carries it with pain. Happy the man who does not have to carry this heavy burden. To him the messages come as a small still voice. And if they insist on thinking that they do it all by themselves, that is all right. It reminds me of a father who picks up a tree trunk together with his three year old son who is 'helping' him. The father goes along with the game, and when they have dragged it away the child says, 'All by myself, eh Dad?'

If you watch carefully you can see 'coincidence' continually at work in your life, right down to small and apparently unimportant details. As when you are looking for a holiday home and you have left it too late. You want to go to a particular area and everything is full. And just as you have almost given up somebody says, 'Hey, we aren't using our home in August, would you like to borrow it?' And moreover it is exactly where you want to be?

Angels? Surely they do not bother about our holidays? But why ever not? We make a totally wrong division between important and unimportant. And between what is solemn and what is not. I was once listening to a lecture given by a wise man, in the vestry of an old and ancient church. He said seriously, 'It feels good to be allowed to speak here, in these hallowed surroundings.' He was silent for a moment and then said, 'I have just come from another holy place. I was having a pee.'

That is pure Zen. Because suddenly you realise that no place is intrinsically holy. That would be idolatry. Nor is any act unholy. At the most you yourself can make it profane.

I am reminded of a very beautiful story of a Zen master who taught his pupils that they must never worship idols. Idolatry was for the ignorant.

One of the pupils passed the open window of his teacher one evening and saw him kneeling in front of a wooden statue of Buddha. He could not contain himself and cried out full of horror, 'Master, what are you doing there?' The teacher looked up, greatly irritated, and said, 'I am paying homage to this statue, just as my ancestors before me, it has been with the family for many years.'

The pupil became very confused by this and walked around for days in a gloomy mood. Then it began to dawn on him that perhaps in exceptional circumstances it might be a good idea to worship statues.

No sooner had he got to this stage of his meditations, than it began to freeze colder than he had ever known it. That evening he walked again past his teacher's window and he heard the sound of wood being chopped. He looked in and saw to his consternation that his master was chopping up the Buddha statue.

Again he could not contain himself and called out anxiously, 'Master, what are you doing now? Your family statue!'

The master looked up with irritation and said, 'How you do keep moaning. I am chopping wood now because I am cold.'

So, holy places, solemnity, it all depends on your attitude and is not tied down to place or occasion. One act is not holier than another act, nor is it more important. Constantly making that mistake can cost us dearly. That is also why some manual workers and businessmen sometimes think that a doctor does holier work than they do themselves because he 'cures people'. (And hence the necessity for as many people as possible studying medicine.) This is delusion. A man who works on the roads and who works with joy in his heart acts in a holier way than a doctor who thinks, 'Just one more patient and I've done for the day.'

That is why I am convinced there are no important or unimportant events for these celestial guides and that holiday homes or a bicycle tour are just as important to them as a cusp in our life, or a healing.

I sincerely hope you all may have known the solution which came to you out of the blue. Many great discoveries have been made that way. You think and think and the solution to a problem escapes you. You put it out of your head and 'hey, presto', there it is! Do you know what that is called nowadays? We have a beautiful new expression: 'The creative capacity of the right half of the brain.' The left half of the brain contains much more the analytical capacity, the practical side of life, whereas artistic expression and inspirations come from the right half.

Well now, I believe that such ideas are really incorrect. It is typical of the twentieth century not to allow someone else the honour and instead, insist on crediting it all to our own precious account. Those few ounces of grey matter a 'creative' organ? How can we think of such a thing? Granted it is one of the greatest wonders of the whole Creation, a starry sky full of cells that radiate in all directions, but creative? No, what we see there is not spontaneous creativity. It is a receiver tuned to an angelic radio station. If we tune in accurately we receive messages and we call them intuition and inspiration. And if someone has the broadcasting part switched on without being aware of it we call it coincidence. But it is not we who organise coincidence, or obtain intuition or inspiration. Neither are they blind forces wandering through the cosmos with which you can do as you like, just as you can sail a boat by using the wind intelligently. No, they are intelligent beings who see to our welfare, just as Houston sees to the welfare of the astronauts. And the fact that it goes wrong for us so often is not their fault but is caused by our not being sufficiently tranquil. Or that we don't listen carefully.

Perhaps, after all these examples and analogies I can go a little further into the question as to what a guardian angel really is. A guardian angel is, just like us, an intelligent and conscious creature made by God. It usually finds itself in a dimension that transcends this world with its three dimensions.

The three dimensions which we inhabit probably also exist in his world, but are contained within his world the way a point is part of a plane.

A guardian angel, which forms a separate category in the world of angels, has the task of being a messenger to those who have descended into time. He also has a duty to protect and carefully guide us, and often he warns us. His signals are probably received by the right half of our brain. But we only hear them when we are quiet inside.

Sometimes an angel appears unexpectedly in this world. Sometimes he looks like a human being, dressed just like everyone around him. Does he have a human appearance in heaven too? I do not think this is a very meaningful question because we cannot easily imagine shapes in a world with more dimensions than are found in our own. We can safely assume that he will be seen as radiant and fearsomely beautiful in heaven. In our world he has to conceal himself behind the cloak of everyday life, otherwise everyone would fall at his feet in worship. But that would be like a dog which rolled on its back for the master it worships. It would limit our freedom. That is why he chooses a simple form.

Angels differ from us, in that they are so completely permeable to God's will, that their deeds express his will completely. That does not appear easy to me.

It seems to me, speaking from a human point of view, a very heavy task for a guardian angel to guide a human being in such a way that the person concerned notices little or nothing. He is permitted to give gentle warnings and nothing else. And only that while he sees his charge stagger from one blunder to the next, switch off his receiver, perpetrate pranks which make good angels hold their breath, in short, live in the way most people live on this planet. It seems to me to be much more frustrating than bringing up a child to whom you can raise your voice from time to time.

But perhaps words such as 'frustrating' and 'holding your breath' are typically human. Perhaps there is only compassion in the world above for the stumbling simple humans.

We need to develop a kind of feeling that will allow us to differentiate between the real and the false stories about guardian angels that are currently circulating. Check your own feeling on the following story which was printed on November 14, 1981 in the Dutch newspaper 'De Telegraaf'. I give a shortened version. It was headed 'Angel at the Wheel'.

In the article we read how a bus carrying fifty-three pilgrims was on its way from the pilgrimage city of Fatima in Portugal to Bilbao in Spain when something remarkable happened. The story is told by Father Don Cesar Trapiello Velez from Leon, who is prepared to swear on the Bible that what he relates is true. It was first published in the Spanish newspaper 'ABC'. While the bus drove along very mountainous terrain with a lot of bends the driver Juan Garcia lost control. The article suggested that this happened because he was overcome by religious ecstasy. The reverend Father Trapiello saw that with his own eyes. Personally, I am of the opinion that another possibility may have been that what Trapiello thought was religious ecstasy could have been sheer terror because the driver lost control through some mechanical fault or other in the bus.

Whatever the case was, while the remaining pilgrims began to shout and cry, the bus lifted itself a little into the air and then began to speed along without collision but with increasing speed. Father Trapiello said it was as if the bus floated on a cushion of air.

After a quarter of an hour the bus stopped against a steep slope, without the brakes having been applied and inside the bus a voice was heard to say that this was the archangel Michael and that what had happened was to be taken as a sign of faith.

The writer of the Dutch article asked himself — though without actually intending to scoff — if the elevated status of St Michael was really compatible with the obvious contempt for Spanish highway codes. And he recalls that the previously mentioned Scottish philosopher David Hume commented in his essay 'Wonders': 'If you can choose, take the least unlikely.' The writer of this article decides that if he has to choose between a reverend Father who lies and an archangel who takes joy-rides, the choice is not really difficult.

If you try to develop a feeling for this story, it seems all wrong.

I do not really know exactly why. Perhaps it is because the whole incident is pointless. If the driver is overcome with religious ecstasy and thus loses control, then the same angel who caused this perilous situation in the first place spends time trying to put things right again. That is not very probable.

When the brakes failed and the angel had to take over then the angel does not have to say that this is a sign of faith. In short, this story seems inconsistent.

But what is much more noticeable is the remark of the reporter who asks himself if the elevated status of St Michael is consistent with the obvious contempt for the Spanish traffic laws. Such a remark makes it obvious that we are living in the post-Christian era. Christianity has always taken the standpoint that the Creator Himself came to earth in the form of His Son to save humanity. For such a Christianity is it not difficult to assume that one of God's servants, the archangel Michael, helps rescue a bus full of people from a perilous situation?

But our enlightened times finds this ridiculous. St Michael is too elevated to worry himself with such trifles, for he has many other worries. In a way we have become so used to great disasters that a bus or two full of pilgrims plunging down a ravine does not really mean all that much to us. And we may well think that it does not matter to St Michael very much either.

This twentieth century is not really an atheist century, as is often asserted. Atheism is a vacuum and nature tends to allow vacuums to be filled within a short period.

No, our time has gone back to a pre-Biblical idea of God. When God was the inaccessible God. The frosty potentate, who did not take any personal interest in his subjects.

The Judeo-Christian world image of a God who cherishes with unending love even the smallest being of His Creation has been replaced by the old Moloch who, seated on high, dealt out disasters and favours so as not to be bored. And although I admit that the Spanish story is, according to David Hume's axiom, probably to be ascribed to a un-truthful Father, the conclusion of a much too exalted St

Michael was so typical of our age that I have dealt with and examined the story at much length.

How did such an attitude really get started? How is it that people lament, 'Man is but dust on this earth and the earth is but a grain of sand in the universe'. I believe that we just have not grown fast enough to match the enormous expansion of our knowledge.

A civilisation in which people think that heaven begins just above your head, as was thought in the Middle Ages, has a totally different outlook to our own, which knows of those millions of light years in the universe. Perhaps that is why we are so closed because we think that God lives so very far away.

That is why it is such a great wonder that just now these angel stories are beginning to appear. Heaven is on the point of breaking through. Everyone should know the story of the Temple of Janus, the ancient God with two heads. In times of disaster and war both front and rear door stood open as a sign that even when the jaws of hell are gaping the way to heaven is wide open.

Again we live in times when hell gapes at our very feet. One has only to read the threat which Soviet Russia directed at Holland on July 27, 1982 which stated that the Soviet Union has the atomic capacity to wipe Holland from the face of the earth. This threat is not based on hollow boasts but is in fact the truth. And that is just the atomic hell, which may cause people to lose their bodies. Far worse are those spiritual straits which tear people's souls apart. Because someone who wants to loose the hounds of war at another person destroys, if only through that intention, something essential inside himself. The armament industry that consumes so many millions of dollars is not only a cancer in any national budget but also a serious sickness of the human soul.

The Temple of Janus is open yet again. Environmental pollution wafts in through the back door while at the front door stand the figures of angels. And those angels are not always saviours. Sometimes their task is merely to lend strength to the person who is about to die.

Jesus was strengthened by an angel in the Garden of Gethsemane, before being martyred and crucified. (Luke 22, verse 43). Ivan Moiseyev, a young Protestant from the Soviet Union, saw a beautiful angel just above him who called out to him not to be afraid. After this he was persecuted mercilessly for his faith and in July 1972 he died a martyr's death at the hands of KGB executioners.

We must now ask ourselves the following:

In this slowly accelerating renaissance of angel stories, are we dealing with something real or with some form of subsidiary psychological event? Something which we can laugh about because it happened to the second cousin once removed of a simple-minded neighbour? Are these the daydreams of the people who feel themselves crushed flat by the immense Juggernaut of a century pregnant with potential disaster?

What kind of creatures are these guardian angels? There are commentaries in the Old Testament which say that the birds created on the Fifth Day were not actually birds but angels. According to the commentary they are a separate creation.

Yet another opinion about angels exists. One of the best exponents of that school of thought was Swedenborg. This Swedish visionary, philosopher and scientist says that originally both heaven and hell were empty but that man himself gradually populated these areas. According to Swedenborg, after death man goes first to an intermediate area, a spiritual world. He remains there in a state which is very similar to life on earth. He experiences his body in much the same way as on earth, and the surroundings are like an earthly landscape.

This description is very similar to the Tibetan idea about the intermediate state of Bardo, and with the description of seriously ill people who have, according to their own words, 'gone for a quick peep up there'.

From this spiritual state people are sent to their permanent dwelling. That is heaven for those who have bound themselves to heaven in the course of their earthly life and hell for those who have taken hell into their souls. They do not go there by way of 'reward' or 'punishment'. No, they go of their own free will to the place which attracts them most, where they feel most at home. A man who eventually lives in heaven is called an angel by Swedenborg and one who lives in hell is called a devil.

In heaven and in hell people join up with particular groups. People who belong together by virtue of common attitudes. And from those groups a certain influence flows towards the people still living on earth. Good inspiration and help from heaven, bad inspiration and temptation from hell.

Here on earth you can choose which particular broadcasts you prefer to hear within your soul, those of the heavenly groups or those of the hellish ones. In this fashion people grow in this present life in the direction of the groups which they will join in the afterlife.

Joy Snell, a nurse whom we will meet again later on in this book, saw many people die, and was able to see quite clearly that people were fetched by angels, and that these were already departed loved ones.

The ideas of Swedenborg and Snell about our guardian angels are, according to my views, extremely refreshing. It makes angels our nearest family. They are much closer to us than the astronauts from other galaxies which are offered us these days as rescuers. A scaly person with an E.T. head can be very engaging, but I cannot really feel any more empathy for it than I would for an overgrown lizard. But an angel who has experienced life on earth and knows the situations that arise on this sublunary world, that is a totally different case. You can love a person like that.

Just suppose you really were part of a celestial company. One part spends time on another world, while the other is still here on earth.

It would explain why you feel you are part of certain people. Even people you have never seen before yet with whom you feel immediate kinship.

Such a celestial company has probably, as one of its tasks, the duty of awakening people on earth who are part of their group. Perhaps you can now look at people in an entirely different way. You start to think, 'Which angel group do you belong to?' Or if you see a brute like Hitler or Stalin, then you might think, 'Which devil have you given birth to?'

And with that I would like to point out a remark that Rudolf Meijer makes in his book 'Man and his Angel'. He said that the false teachings of materialism have had such a pernicious influence on the spirit, that even the angels intimately connected with a person can be sucked in and 'fall again' in a manner of speaking. I do not know if Meijer is right but I think we should face this possibility.

That means that man not only carries on his shoulders a tremendous responsibility for his life on earth but also for the Kingdom of God.

It would mean that not only are we protected but that we also have to protect. As grown-up children have to protect their parents when they have grown old. And even if angels do not grow old, their love for us makes them just as vulnerable as parents are to children. For this reason we should look after them.

Summing it all up what I would like to say about guardian angels is that they are much nearer to us than would at first have been thought. That they appear to us from time to time as ordinary people because they have been ordinary people themselves. And that they understand us particularly well because they are related to us.

Once they shared our fears, our uncertainties, our less

attractive characteristics. They are not semi-abstract, totally sexless, pale and wan beings. They are perfected through suffering.

At least, if what Swedenborg says is true. But even if Swedenborg is not right, and angels are a separate creation, then it should still fill us with hope that they appear to us in human form. Because in a world of truth, form and being are identical. There nobody can appear as a human being to whom humanity is alien.

We are therefore surrounded by legions of helpful and very closely related beings. There are (in heaven) more people concerned for us than there are (on earth) working against us. That is a good antidote to all those notions of doom.

Ponder well: Because you are human it is just as certain that you have a guardian angel as it is certain that you were born from a mother. If God looks at you He will see two walking, not one.

3. Archangels and Angel Princes

In the Dionysian system (of which more below), guardian angels are placed immediately next to the earth. They stand beside man and regularly cross the border between 'There' and 'Here and now'.

They also only deal with one single person. You have the right to talk about 'my' guardian angel, as long as the word 'my' does not imply personal property.

What I am about to do in the following chapters is to take the reader over little known territory. In the middle of the first century A.D. there lived in Athens a man called Dionysius the Areopagite. He was called that because he was a member of the Athens court of justice, which gathered on the Areopagus.

He was converted to Christianity by Paul and died a martyr's death.

To him are attributed a number of writings which first became well-known in the sixth century. It is now thought that these are derived from a neo-Platonic philosopher of the fifth century but one must bear in mind that the truth was mostly passed down orally for many centuries before being eventually written down.

So it is quite possible that the writings ultimately derive from Dionysius. In any case, he is the one who organised the already long-existing angel hierarchies.

It is his system, which for many centuries has been the standard one in the church, that I shall stick to for the present. Therefore, when you ask, 'Where does he get that from?' I will call on the insight of that early Christian

6 Just as the rings encircle Saturn, so the first
heaven encircles our visible creation

martyr. Obviously I will add many ideas of my own on the subject. Because you must try to combine that which was known in older days with the reality of the present. What follows is thus his system combined with my commentaries.

I have also combined his system with the teachings of the four worlds which we come across in ancient Hebrew thinking. This seemed to result in a specially fruitful combination.

Here we start climbing to greater heights. Look on me as a guide to the church tower. Mind the steps and try not to bump your head; off we go!

As I have said, Archangels stand one step higher. In this system they are indicated as ruling over a city.

Angel Princes have a whole country under their rule. First of all we must discuss the world in which these beings find themselves. Guardian angels, archangels, angel princes, i.e., those watching over people, areas and nations, live in a world which is different from our own.

In the ancient system of knowledge our world was called the world of doing. We have almost made it a world of Doom and that is a tragic development, because doing meant something very special. It means to beautify, to decorate. Completing something which is to all intents finished but needs a festive touch. As when a woman adorns the festive table with flowers and beautifully polished silver.

The world lying behind our visible creation was called the world of formation. The matrix, as it were, out of which our visible world has come into existence. If everything which we can perceive with our five senses is a cake, then the invisible mould that defines the form is the baking tin. Then it becomes easy to understand why it is that with a limited number of cake tins you can bake a virtually unlimited number of cakes. Perhaps it explains the enormous quantity and growth which we perceive around us.

The world inhabited by the angels also has very different properties from those of our own. In the first place it is much more malleable. It is not all that difficult to imagine that world since every person who dreams during the night finds himself in such regions. And everyone knows how changeable form can be in a dream. The face of an unknown man changes into that of my son, a familiar house suddenly has different rooms, a car changes into a bicycle during the ride. To all intents and purposes it seems as if the matter of that area obeys our feelings and thoughts. Everything you think appears as a form in front of you. It is also the area to which we go after our death. That is why you cannot keep your thoughts secret. Everything is revealed all around you, as Lorber showed in his books. That would explain why the reports from people who have had a glimpse 'around the corner' differ so much. A person full of hate and resentment will encounter a different world from that which someone who is full of love and warmth will find. The Tibetan Book of the Dead says that you can meet up with fearsome monsters, but that those are nothing other than your own soul's attitudes made visible. When you shut your eyes you see the very first beginnings of that world. Endless variations of grey and black which are continually subject to kaleidoscopic changes.

A second characteristic of this formative world (known in Hebrew as Yetsirah, from which the word for potter is derived) is the different way that time is experienced. In the present, time is a line on which we experience the 'now' as a point. Over there it is possible to view the line as a whole.

One of my patients who lay drowning after an accident, said, 'I saw my whole life pass by.'

In all probability this was 'corrected' afterwards. Because we do not recognise in the present the idea of seeing everything all at once, we say, 'It passed by me in a flash.' But it is more probable that it appears complete before your eyes, as in a picture gallery.

A third factor also has to do with time. Time 'there' is not completely absent, but it passes in a different way. A thousand years in this world are but a day and a night there — just twenty-four hours. If you were to compare our world with the blueprint of a house, in which every inch represents several feet, then this world may be compared to the map of a country on which every inch represents a number of miles. The basic time unit 'there' is different. And that has to do with the subject of this chapter, the archangels and the angel princes. For example, the two thousand years between the birth of Christ and now is but a mere two days to them. To us the last appearance of a really important angel like Gabriel happened so long ago that we are even doubting whether such a being ever existed. To Gabriel it seems like the day before yesterday that he called on Mary. We must be conscious of that at all times when we think about these friends of mankind. In our awareness they may be legends, while to them a human lifetime seems just a passing flash. I suspect that when they are guiding and leading our world they have to adjust their attention before they can perceive us. They have to modify their awareness tremendously and I think such manipulation is a great sacrifice.

It is remarkable that humanity has always known of the existence of such elevated beings, yes, has even known a number of them by name. As our true leaders they are intensely involved with humanity's destiny and they play a deciding role during moments of crisis. I want to tell you a little more about some of these old friends of humanity. But first I would like you to ask yourselves if you have ever noticed that every city has its own guiding archangel.

Now I assume that you are no more clairvoyant than I am. Were you clairvoyant, you might exclaim, 'Surely everyone sees that!' I know such people do exist, but most of us are not clairvoyant. How then would you notice the influence of such an archangel? Now you must agree with me that every city has its own character. That character is not just the lowest common denominator of all those who live there. It is rather the other way round: someone who has lived for a long time in a certain city or community takes on part of the character of that city.

Take the two towns of Amsterdam and Rotterdam. Comparable in size and yet, what a difference! And it is not just a matter of different football teams. It is not all that easy to explain the difference. You can 'taste' it as you come into the town. As I am a citizen of neither Amsterdam nor Rotterdam, I will not even attempt to explain the differences, since I do not want to provoke cries of indignation.

I would merely like to state that there is more to the general atmosphere than just what is created by the people who live there. That the destiny of the one city differs totally from that of the other (one has only to remember the terrible suffering of Rotterdam in 1940) and that cannot be explained on purely rational grounds. You could almost say that the angel of Amsterdam has an excitable character whereas the angel of Rotterdam is a little more composed. Because angels, just like people, have their own characters and their own typical features.

'A real Amsterdammer,' we say of someone. Why, and what would happen if he moved away?

As soon as a city or a region has its own character, remember that this is more than just a vague feeling. It is the inspiration and leadership of the ruling archangel that are being felt. Perhaps I saw the imprint of the one who guards the Kennemerland country in those clouds on that autumn day during the war.

Now we go up one more step.

Angel princes rule over whole countries and nations, and their characters are even more pronounced. If the archangels express themselves in a regional dialect which can still be understood by other people in that country, then you will perceive that angel princes rule over a people bound together by a language that those of an adjacent country often cannot comprehend.

And what differences of character between those peoples. Take the English and the French, or the Italians and the Germans. It is not a question of hereditary traits, because a family that moves into such a country often takes on the colouring of that country within a single generation.

I wonder whether angel princes are bound to a particular region so that the individual moving into such a region comes under his influence, or whether he is bound to a group of people. I suspect that he belongs to a region, a part of this globe. In that case the angel prince of the North Americas would be the same as that of the Red Indians. The continual, restless wanderings of many American citizens would thus be a 'Red Indian trait'. I have noticed that my American friends are astonished whenever they hear that I have lived in the same house for thirty years.

The coats of arms of different countries could possibly be connected to their angel princes. The German eagle, the Dutch lion, the rising sun of Japan, the hammer and sickle of the Russians which, if looked at carefully, is nothing less than the crescent-moon and star of the Middle East region, they are all astrological symbols. They point clearly to heaven and not to the earth.

Our real rulers are therefore quite different from those we read about in the papers. Happy the people whose earthly rulers know this and who say that they rule 'by the Grace of God'.

After having mused over what the Dionysius' system would mean in these times, I would now like to give a description of some of the higher angels which are known by name. These angels have functions other than just looking after the interests of cities and nations. They include all of mankind in their comprehensive tasks.

Michael

The first is Michael, the one whom Daniel called 'the great prince', who 'standeth for the children of thy people'. (Daniel 12, verse 1) Thus Michael is the prince of Israel, but not just that! He rules over much more than just the region around Palestine. His territory includes all those people who say that their kingdom is not of this earth. You could call him a super-angel. One who has risen above cities and regions and nations to the function of helping all those who feel themselves to be pilgrims, or strangers on this earth.

The earliest report known to me about the angel Michael is not to be found in the Bible but in ancient Eygptian mythology. Here I must point out that Michael is sometimes depicted in old paintings as holding a pair of scales on which a man and a woman are weighed. Where does the idea come from? Apparently it was an idea that was once prevalent. Well, that weigher of souls is not unknown in the history of the human race. In Egypt people believed that after death the soul was transported to Anubis. He laid the heart of the dead person on one scale of the balance and put a feather as counter-weight on the other scale. The Bible also mentions the idea (Proverbs 21, verse 2) that God weighs a person's heart.

Anubis was depicted amongst the gods of Egypt as a god with the head of a dog or a jackal. This did not mean that he really had such a head but that he had something to do with the most important star in Egypt, Sirius, the Dog Star. Our 'dog days' (23 July to 23 August) are derived from this.

Anubis was thus a sort of symbol standing for Sirius, although it might be better to say that both Sirius and Anubis were associated with the underlying spiritual reality. On winter nights you can clearly see the star Sirius under the constellation of Orion. It seems that the star Sirius clearly points in the direction of an angel prince. The name Sirius is related to the Hebrew word 'Sar', which means commander or prince. In Persian the star Sirius is called Tistar, which means chief. In old Akkadian the word for Sirius is Kasista which means leader or prince.

Summing it all up: Michael is well known as the commander of the heavenly legions. He is depicted as the weigher of people. Anubis is a weigher of people's hearts. Through his dog's head he is connected to Sirius and words like commander, prince and chief.

It is thus highly probable that the Israelites, the Eygptians, the Persians and the Akkadians all knew the same mighty angel prince and that is the one we call Michael.

It is also noticeable that Michael is connected, via Sirius and Anubis, with the hottest part of the year known as the Dog Days. Michael is always there where the fighting is fiercest. He is a tireless champion for a good cause.

What does it in fact mean, that Michael weighs souls? Let us take another look at that ancient symbol of Anubis — the heart on one scale of the balance, the feather on the other.

The symbol is really very simple. Have you ever been really angry? How heavy your footsteps sound on the ground. Or ever lain, worried out of your mind? Your mattress feels like concrete under the weight of your body. Have you ever really loved a person? Then you feel so light that you could be floating.

What is being weighed by Anubis is the lightness in your heart. So really the question is: How much love did you give? Actually, how much love did you pass on? Because love flows to us from heaven and we have to transfer it to the earth.

When we shuffle off this mortal body, the love-filled soul whirls upwards like a feather, the heavy egotistical soul falls like a brick. In the old Jewish Temple stood an altar for burned offerings. Animals were burned as a sacrifice. And on that spot, the south side of the temple, Michael was placed. He is present when the earthly body vanishes and the true nature of the soul appears. Again in that temple he stands close by the fire, the place of a fiery warrior. The earliest mention of Michael that I know of in the Bible, is in the tenth chapter of the book of Daniel. The prophet goes through an incredible experience. He meets the Lord in person and the Lord tells him a very strange story. Here I relate the content of the story rather than quote it word for word. He says to Daniel, 'Three weeks ago I noticed that you tried to get in touch with me and I immediately came to help you. But the prince of the Persians has held me up all this time. Fortunately Michael came to my aid, and so the struggle went the right way.'

Now that is, if you think about it, an absurd situation. Just imagine the Creator of heaven and earth being resisted by one of His own creations, albeit the angel prince of Persia. (A ruler who operated under the sign of the Ram, as we can read elsewhere in Daniel.) And that it is Michael, another angel prince, who can relieve the siege. What a situation, and where is God's almighty power?

And then we see the Creator's character described in all its detail. First comes the question, 'Are not all angel princes good? Whatever got into the prince of the Persians?'

There are such things as fallen angels. Woe betide the nation which is ruled by such an angel prince. Then you have to deal with an Ayatolla Khomeiny or an Idi Amin. Why that happens to a nation is something I do not know; these things are the tremendous secrets of this Creation. Whatever the reason, the prince of the Persians was evil. As far as that is concerned, the story is applicable to the present situation. But good or bad, the rule is that God gives freedom to all creatures with their own conscious individuality, be they people, angels or angel princes. Zeus or Odin would have annihilated the miscreant prince of the

Persians with fiery lightning the moment he said, 'You cannot come through here.' But it is a characteristic of the living God to control himself on such an occasion and to wait. Because His final goal is the salvation of the entire Creation. A community of souls who love each other totally. Not a pack of dogs who wag their tails as they crouch before Him on the ground. That is why He needs creatures who rally to His support both in the heavenly regions and on earth. One free will set against another. Only that way is it fair. Michael thus immediately distinguishes himself as the one who stands up for the 'underdog'. What have we here, we ask, God as underdog?

Certainly, and it is said in all humility. God knowingly and willingly ties both hands behind his back and then confronts a heavily-armed ruler. It is, of course, true that the ruler derives each and every ounce of power from the one who stands bound before him, but he simply chooses to forget this. God does not in any way diminish the power of the angel prince, no, in fact, He allows him the power to resist Him. That is how Daniel describes the situation. It is as if a small child is rude to his father, and the father just watches him silently, and then suddenly another child jumps up in his defence. Are these not situations that constantly arise in our daily lives? In fact, it is really sad to learn in the course of this story that not one solitary person determinedly took God's part, except for Michael.

'Your prince Michael,' says God to Daniel; Prince of Israel. It is a good idea to go into all this in greater detail since it concerns us all. When we think of Israel then we ought to remember that this name was given to Jacob after he had wrestled all night long with an angel.

Wrestling with an angel seems to be another possibility. But what is that other than a spiritual battle? And Jacob came out of that struggle with a new name. According to ancient ways of thinking, it meant he was changed, became another person. However, he did not leave the struggle undamaged, for he limped afterwards.

We are told little about the details of that struggle. It is certain that it has some connection with Jacob's justified fear of the brutal Esau, who had sworn to kill him and who was on his way with a small army. We see here a man in fear for his life and with a choice of only two possibilities. Either he once again finds one of his clever solutions, as he had done so often before in his life, or he gives up the struggle and entrusts himself entirely to God. In my opinion that was the subject of his spiritual struggle. And that is also the struggle for many who take life seriously, who have to live with themselves. Whomsoever is drawn into that struggle belongs to Israel.

And Michael is the ruler of those people. He is the ruler of the lonely struggler. In these times, with the really crushing attack on the freedom of the individual there are still people here and there, alone or in groups, fighting to keep up human dignity. They have to take up the fight against unwieldy authorities, or against inhuman bureaucracies.

Some struggle against the might of money. And every now and then you see that a small group fighting against the titans gains a victory. As though a pigmy trips up a giant. Such as when Solzhenitsyn drove the Russian authorities to despair. Or when ordinary citizens try to prevent the murder of seals on the icy wastes of Canada. So many examples can be found in our own times.

And the rule is that Michael takes the part of those people who find themselves in dire straits, such as is mentioned in the twelfth chapter of Daniel. Daniel states there that there will come a time of great oppression for this world such as never existed before and that at that time the great prince Michael will be active once more. When that will be is not precisely known. From that same chapter twelve of the book of Daniel, a number of biblical researchers have deduced that this could well be the twentieth century. It would be taking us too far from the subject of this book to take this any further, but many signs do seem to indicate this century.

Do not imagine that salvation is a streamlined process. A safety valve on a pressure cooker. A stride from victory to victory. No, Michael and suffering go hand in hand. After all, did I not tell you that Michael stood 'at the side of the sacrificial altar'? Right at the spot where the flesh went up in smoke. How should we explain that?

If we look at our existence here on earth, then it is clear that we are not here for the fun of it. The candle of life is soon burned, each day leaves us with less, and the passage of time is a painful process. People we love grow old before our eyes and die. Or — and that is worse — people we love become estranged from us and we lose track of them. Satisfied desires leave the taste of ashes in the mouth and our labours lead to nothing.

Last year I treated a small boy for an allergic condition. After a few ups and downs I was able to gain the satisfaction of seeing the child bloom again. Later he was drowned in a pond.

Good intentions lead nowhere and friendships crumble. Time erodes all, like the fire on the altar consuming the sacrifical animal. And yet Michael stands there at its side. What does it all mean?

It means that something durable is being brewed in the process. That which perished was only the part that was too weak for eternity. Michael is concerned with burning off the transient so as to allow the permanent to shine forth. He stands at the precise point where earthly things are drawn through their zero point. How is that to be explained? It can be seen as the freeing of a homeopathic medicine from the shackles of matter. You simply dilute it so much that matter falls away and the real essence of the medicine remains.

We are all negatives of photographs that are waiting to be developed. I think that the corrosive fluids which are required do not feel very pleasant to the photographic paper assuming that it had feelings. But the result is that you can separate the light from the dark.

That fiery side of Michael is not easy to understand. Inside every human being the real person is hidden, but hidden so deeply that he cannot even recognise himself. It is as if a fireproof gold figure is packed in stiffly wound straw. You can just about see that it is supposed to represent a human being, but that is all. But now we throw the whole thing into the fire. The fire of pain, loneliness and death. And as the straw burns, the original intention of the sculptor appears. The form becomes more and more distinct, as you see with some older people who have led a long and good life. Sometimes, when you meet the people in their old age — so full of warmth, love and real goodness — and you happen to chance on a photograph of them taken forty years earlier, you can be amazed. Was this beautiful old person hidden in that exterior? How is it possible? All hardness had gone.

These are all clumsy attempts to show you Michael. The analogies will not hold water, there are too many exceptions. I am aware of that. But perhaps in this way I can show you a little of the great archangel who, as we get to know him better, seems more and more to be the angel of our own time. Because our time is so caught up in the spell of transience, that we have become full of despair and try to drug ourselves in order not to notice that everything passes. In the last instance, the quest of our time is not the search for more energy or greater social security but rather for a more meaningful life. And that too is something about which the elderly can teach us a lot. Those old people who we prefer to put away in one of the many homes we have created specially for them.

I always have a lot of admiration for older people who dedicate themselves to some task even though they are close to death. My old preacher was reading a very complicated book on psychology with great difficulty, in order to keep up with things. My old grandfather sat at the table with a textbook on plants so as to identify a particular specimen. An old lady, the same one as was snatched away from in front of the old Blue Tram, was working her embroidery with utmost precision. They all know that their essence lies in something that cannot be grasped or held onto here. That the loving gesture, or the involvement with the work itself are the real essence. That eternity can be part of every human act. Yes, even in that very last meaningful act — letting go of the last breath.

All this is the terrain of Michael, the dragon slayer. For the dragon stands for the imprisonment of matter, the desire to give material objects a lasting character. As, for instance, those false ideologies that seek to make a lasting Utopia here on earth. As if you can make anything durable here on earth, with the possible exception of a skeleton. Perhaps that is why the totalitarian regimes of this century have murdered so mercilessly, since their followers knew within their hearts that durability can be found only on the other side of the grave.

Michael is thus the inexorable opponent of Satan, he who tried to make of man a materialist. The controversy between these two has lasted since the beginning of creation if we are to believe the old stories.

In the apocryphal gospel of Bartholomew we are told that God created man in his image using clay that Michael fetched from the four corners of the earth. And that when man was ready, the (at that time not yet evil) angel passed by. 'This', said Michael, 'is God's image and we must therefore pay homage to it.'

'I, the first angel God ever made, should pay homage to that lump of clay?' asked the evil one indignantly. 'Never!'

'You will be in trouble if you go on like that,' said Michael. But the evil angel rebelled, and with him many other angels; that was the beginning of all evil.

This story strengthens the rumour that the fall of the angels had something to do with the creation of man. And it is extremely noticeable that, at a later stage, and throughout his complete history, man has been more attracted to the fallen angels and all their evil, than to the side of good. He is more akin to evil than to good, and God has been courting man ever since, rather like a rejected suitor does a capricious young woman.

How many people have depicted that rebellion of the angels at some time or another. Michael with his shining suit of armour, and Lucifer, already partly changed into a dragon, falling to earth from heaven. In legends Michael lives on as St George, the dragon slayer. The brave knight with his long fierce sword standing on a squirming beast.

The short epistle of Jude from the New Testament also contains a story about Michael. It is a strange story, which tells of how Michael quarrelled with the devil about the body of Moses and that he did not dare to 'bring against him a railing accusation' but said, 'The Lord rebuke thee.'

What sort of story is that? An archangel and man's old enemy arguing about the body of Moses? But what is the body of the prophet other than the teaching he has left us: The Torah.

If we look at everything from this point of view we can understand the quarrel much better. Because it has always been the case that good and wise teachings are corrupted with the passage of time. Little by little they are changed by all sorts of interpretations to mean the contrary. The gentle pressure of loving persuasion used by St Paul changes after only a few centuries into the harsh compulsion and tortures of the Inquisition. The suggestion that all should subject themselves to the guidelines of the authorities, as set out in Romans chapter thirteen, was quickly taken up by every government and used as a licence for slavery.

These things do not happen by themselves. The evil and very intelligent powers feel themselves threatened by love and will always try to push loving laws to such an extreme that people start to curse those laws and throw out the baby with the bath water.

You only have to see what the nineteenth century did with the subject of sex in our lives. They made it into something unclean and objectionable, even something dirty. And all that with the Bible in one hand and a pious expression. No wonder that our century has broken loose sexually. That is however not excusable, since extremes are never good and do not lead to happiness.

Making people unhappy while holding the Bible, the Bible which is nothing other than a love letter from God to his people, was something that Michael saw coming. He saw the corruption that was to come, and he disputed with the devil over whether he had the right to do that. But — and it is extremely mysterious — he did not dare go any further. It is just as if each time corruption is once again permitted by the highest spiritual authority to be found in heaven. Just as the disasters which overcame Job were permitted. Apparently it is all part of a gigantic plan of which we see only the results.

Sometimes we can understand a little of why this should be so. For the consequences of corruption on this earth are terrible. An ocean of suffering and pain accompanies humanity on its painful journey. However, if we look at those lives in which there has been much pain and suffering, then we see that we are dealing with people who have a measure of wisdom about them, and a tolerance. They have understanding for others who have foundered in this morass. And we can also see that lives which have run very smoothly deliver some unbearably upright citizens. Upright in their own eyes, of course. As if the absence of disaster is to be ascribed to a superfluity of bourgeois integrity.

I have noticed, as a matter of fact, that we lack an important word in our language. We know a number of words which begin with 'ego-' and which often have negative associations because they refer to or indicate a part of yourself described by the remainder of the word. We know words like egoistic, egocentric, egotistic. The missing word should be egosacred. Defining somebody who has declared himself holy in his own lifetime, usually through lack of contrary opinions. And in order to break all that 'ego', corruption is permitted once more from time to time, just as indigestion is with those who eat too much rich food.

Yes, I understand a little of why Michael is required by a higher authority to restrain himself, but what a lot that must have cost that combative hero.

Up to this point we have followed Michael on his path through ancient times, but now we have come to the beginning of our own era. And something happens now that fundamentally changes the history of mankind. That applies to everyone on this planet. You can see for instance that when a dyed in the wool communist signs a decree stating that the Christmas story is an outright lie and that Jesus never existed, he still has to date it. And that is done using a date based on the birth of Him whom he denies with all his being. It is the same ridiculous situation that existed between God and the ruler of the Persians.

Michael was closely involved in this event. Dr Bullinger, one of the most brilliant bible researchers of the last century, has discovered, after painstaking research, the precise date of Jesus' birth. He started out using a number of important known facts such as the priestly offices of Abia to which Zacharias, the father of John the Baptist belonged, the six-month age difference between John the Baptist and Jesus, the Census and a few other matters, and he came to a surprising conclusion. He discovered that what we celebrate on December 25 is not the birth of Jesus but his conception.

His very incarnation into matter. And what we call the Christmas story, the birth of Jesus that is, took place some nine months later on September 29. In the year of nativity that was the first day of the Feast of the Tabernacles.

He says then: Two great ones of the Kingdom of Heaven were chosen to guide these two events. Gabriel announced the conception on December 25 when he appeared to Mary. Michael announced the birth on September 29 when he appeared before the shepherds. He is not actually mentioned by name but a remarkable fact points to it having been he and no one else who led the heavenly legions on those fields of Efrata. And that fact is that here in the west Michael has his own feast day. And his feast day is September 29 which is called the feast of Michael and all Angels. (Anyone who wants to follow the precise calculations is referred to appendix 179 of the Companion Bible.)

I have stood on the fields of Efrata and even now, after nearly 2000 years, a soft glow still seems to lie over the landscape. As if a little bit of heaven has been left behind.

We have now seen Michael in a variety of roles. The restrained, self-controlled berater of Satan. The fiery adversary of the ruler of the Persians. The weigher of souls. The slayer of dragons. The announcer of great happiness. We know him from the Book of Revelation as the mighty one who drove out the devil and his associates with a shining sword.

But the Apocalypse of St Paul, also one of the apocryphal books, shows a quite different side to him.

Paul is shown the souls who have stubbornly refused to accept the good on this earth. They find themsleves in torment after their death. For he who embraces evil on earth finds evil as his natural environment after death.

And those souls now see Michael and say, 'We acknowledge that we have done wrong. Have mercy on us, Michael.'

100

And then Michael gives a moving answer. He says, 'I pray without ceasing for the people on this earth but they go on doing evil. If they do just a little bit of good I will protect them. And you people here, weep and I shall weep with you and perhaps God will have mercy on you.' Little wonder this request was honoured by God.

Here we see a very warm emotional angel, and it is good to realise this. Paintings often show angels as rather impassive beings, filled by a clear but cool light. I believe this image appears to be wrong. Here we see one of the greatest of the angels and he is warm and understanding and he hopes fervently for mercy and comfort for the people on earth.

Eternal doom is an invention of people who are little inclined to forgive. Michael demonstrates that he has hope even for the person in hell. If you are not all that good a person yourself, this should be a comforting thought.

We now take a giant leap of 2000 years and arrive in our own time. Where is Michael nowadays? The whole of Christianity has admired and honoured him for centuries. Brilliant works of art have been dedicated to him. A feast has been dedicated to him. And now in the twentieth century we have silence.

Is there anyone amongst my readers who knew that September 29 was his feast? Well, you knew more than I did before I started on my researches. Where is he, this ancient champion of the underdog? Has he forgotten us?

In America there is a preacher who says that he has met Michael. He describes him as a very large martial figure with eyes like pools of fire and a tremendous radiation of love and compassion. According to Buck he looks like a man aged twenty-five with flaxen hair, fine features and with a skin the colour of beaten copper. He is dressed in a white cloak with gold stitching and with a broad gold belt.

Formerly, if I had read such an item I would have thought, 'They stop at nothing over there in America to fill their churches.' But from the book that was written about Buck it appears that he had kept the story quiet and that somebody else had found out about it by accident and told it to others. That keeping quiet sounds very much like the experiences I had of people during my survey. Buck's story could well be based on truth.

He says that Michael is the leader of the struggle against the powers of darkness who are making a determined effort in this century to gain control over this planet.

He is the leader in a battle. That seems to call to mind something not unlike angel armies. Do such things exist? Did Jesus speak the literal truth rather than a parable when He, while being taken prisoner, told Peter that if He wanted to He could have at His disposal twelve legions of angels? (Matthew 26, verse 53)

I find the book written by Buck strange, and if you were to read it you might find the same. Fortunately, his daughter Sharon has written a book about her late father which shows that the Reverend Buck was a genuine man of God, and we seem to be dealing with real events. Angel armies have actually been seen in this century. It is a famous event and it heralds the apocalyptic part of our twentieth century.

The story I am about to tell you occurred during World War I. The German army, after a tremendous bombardment, started moving towards some British trenches to the south-east of Lille. The British soldiers then saw something peculiar. One moment there was the noise of the artillery barrage and the sight of an onrushing enemy, and the next moment the barrage ceased and they saw the Germans flee in total disorder.

The British immediately sent out patrols and they took a number of German officers prisoner. These men had a bewildered look on their faces and told an incredible story: Just as they were moving up under cover of their barrage, the Germans suddenly saw an army looming up on the

British side, clad in white and riding white horses. The first reaction of the Germans was to think that new Moroccan troops had been sent in, and they started pumping shells and bullets from their cannons and machine guns into the oncoming force.

Not a man fell from his horse and then they clearly saw that in front of the army rode a great figure with gold blond hair and a halo round his head. He too was seated on a white horse.

Panic and fear gripped the Germans and they broke off their extremely dangerous offensive. The British, however, had seen nothing, but in the days that followed, dozens of fresh prisoners confirmed the incident. At a later date the event was recorded in both British and German annals and is still well-known as the miracle of the white cavalry of Ypres.

Again I can hear several critics carping, 'Why were the British favoured? A cavalry of angels with Michael at the head fighting on the side of the British? Surely that is beyond belief? Is it simply that the English are so mad about St George and the dragon?'

But is it really so unrealistic.

It is very clear that in this century some countries are much more in the grip of evil than others. And that a permanent victory by such a country over the rest of our planet would set back the development of human history for some hundreds of years.

Just imagine that the barbarian Nazis had conquered the whole world. The gas ovens would have burned first for all Jews, then for all Christians and finally for everyone who was undesirable. A planet held in thrall for hundreds of years, with the blond beast as sole ruler.

Or imagine that Idi Amin had not been chased away but had conquered all of Africa; maybe a return to cannibalism and cruelty of the worst kind.

Or just imagine that communism really gained power over

the entire world, an event that still appears distinctly possible. An eventual eradication of our view of heaven. A Gulag-archipelago on a planetary scale. Such a disaster would be incomprehensible. Humanity would regress, through the use of all the available psychological and chemical aids as well as downright terror, into dull slavery. For communism is that power which has sworn to reckon once and for all with metaphysical man. It sees man as simply a cog in the whole, as an economic labour unit. It denies the heavenly part in man and with it his humanity. It has sworn to eradicate metaphysical man root and branch. That is why it will lose the fight, for the essence of human history lies in man's heavenly task and not in his economic usefulness.

That is why angels are also fighting communism once again. There is an authentic story of the Vietcong who wanted to attack a village and eliminate all Christians. The Christians fled to a church and began to pray. For two days nothing happened. Then the Vietcong slowly went away. A Vietcong prisoner taken at a later date told of how they had not dared to attack the village as it had been surrounded by a whole army of soldiers clad in white.

World War II also showed us glimpses of angel armies. The rescue of the British Expeditionary Force from France is still called the miracle of Dunkirk and then there is the Battle of Britain. One of the people in my survey told me the following story: She has a friend who fought in World War II as a combat pilot in the Battle of Britain. That battle was later seen to be the turning point, and it was from then on that Hitler began to lose the war.

This friend told her that World War II was so much a struggle between good and evil that even the dead flew along to help in the battle.

I did not understand what she meant by this until some time later I read Billy Graham's book 'Angels, God's Secret

Agents'. The story comes from Air Chief Marshall Lord Dowding who tells us that planes whose crews had been killed simply fought on, and that other pilots saw figures sitting in the pilot's seat.

This story confirms the story of my interviewee. Only the way the Air Marshall interpreted that story was different. He was of the opinion that the angels were fighting alongside. This story brings our thoughts back to a distant past when Elisha was in the city of Dothan.

The king of Aram, who had been more than a little annoyed by the way Elisha penetrated all his battle strategy, discovered the prophet's abode and surrounded the city. Early that morning the servant of Elisha got up and saw the mighty host around the city. He was scared senseless and ran up to Elisha who said, 'Don't be afraid because those who are with us are more numerous than those with them.' And as Elisha prayed, the servant suddenly saw the other world and how the whole mountain was surrounded by fiery horses and chariots (2 Kings 6, verse 15). Of course the story has a happy ending for Elisha and his servant. I have taken Elisha's words as the motto for my book as they apply to the lives of individuals as much as to whole nations.

The history of this world has meaning and leads somewhere, and the powers that guide it are not afraid of confrontation, for out of clashes the new is often born.

But if the barbarians threaten victory then it seems necessary to take over for a moment; the heavenly referee blows his whistle momentarily.

This world is not what it seems. Now and then, under special circumstances, the veil is lifted briefly and then we can see an archangel in all his glory.

Oral Roberts, the American faith healer and later the head of the university named after him in Tulsa, Oklahoma, gets his students to mentally absorb a number of slogans. One of these reads, 'Expect a miracle.'

Well, with Michael around we can expect nothing else. And the fact that he is close by could be confirmed by a remarkable fact quite apart from the signs over the centuries.

After the war a congress of German preachers was held. They discovered that — although the name was not a favourite family name — many of them had called their sons Michael.

It is almost as if the shadow cast by Michael falls across this century and that many people feel this intuitively and call their sons after him. This also appears to be the case with one of the great post-war novels, Tolkien's mighty epic 'The Lord of the Rings'. In the East stands a mighty power which cannot be defeated by force of arms. The West is threatened more and more but is aided. The leader of the forces of good is Gandalf. He is older than anyone can imagine; actually he is immortal. He has a fiery character, he is tender as a father though unbribable in a time when even the great commit treachery. He rides a great white horse, is clad in shining white and wears a famous sword at his side, called Glamdring.

It is clear that Tolkien has taken the angel Michael as an example in his prophetic work. And fortunately the armies of Gandalf win the struggle against evil, even if it is by the skin of their teeth.

This was the description of one of the real leaders of humanity. Great dictators, of which so many appear these days, are ridiculous marionettes on the stage of humanity. With their wooden faces they prance on the boards, while their victims endure modern slavery.

No, our true guides look quite different. They are clothed with real power, even if they use if sparingly and in all humility. For they know that their powers are merely borrowed, that they are only passing on light radiating from the Creator Himself. The more the one in authority realises that he rules 'by the grace of God', the more he will be able to give real guidance. And the more he thinks that he does it all himself with the aid of his oligarchy, his junta or his rotten companions, the more he is is a plaything without free will of the powers which rule him totally but without his knowledge. And that is not the mild rule of Michael. It is possession by the evil spirits which are still active in the heavenly regions.

Michael's name is Hebrew. Mi-Ka-El means 'Who (is) as God'. Every person who asks that in utter amazement and reverence stands in the light of Michael's radiance. Even if he is afraid and restless, he will gain the courage to be able to say to himself, 'I am a hero'.

8 A world with such a strong light that we cannot
see it directly — the corona of the sun during
an eclipse

Gabriel

Angel names should end in 'el' since that means God in Hebrew. In fact, angels always refer to God. However exalted they may be, they do not expect or wish for worship. 'Do not look at me, I am but a servant, look at Him!' they say.

Sometimes one of them says, 'Do not listen to Him, look at me!' That is a fallen angel.

Gabriel is derived from the word 'gibor' and that means power or hero. From this word gibor is derived the word geber, a man. Gabriel thus means God's might.

Gabriel is also an old familiar friend of humanity. Again Daniel was the first one to mention him. The old prophet had a terrifying vision 2500 years ago. He saw a tremendous ram bucking to the west, the north and to the south, and no animal could stand up to that ram until eventually he was overcome by a he-goat from the west after a wild struggle. It is Gabriel who explains to Daniel the meaning of this vision (Daniel 8). The ram is the empire of the Medes and Persians that is finally overcome by the Greeks, after a series of victories elsewhere.

Once more you see the astrological symbols of ram and goat being used to symbolise nations. The symbols describe the characteristics of their angel rulers. It is remarkable how relevant this story of the savage bucking of the Persian ram is to our own times.

We see Gabriel again in the ninth chapter of Daniel. He comes in haste and prophesies to Daniel the coming of the Messiah (Daniel 9, verses 21 – 26). And 500 years later, Gabriel does the same again, but this time to Mary.

The real name for angel is 'messenger' and this is the way Gabriel conducts himself. My teacher tells me that according to Jewish tradition, Gabriel stood on the north side of the Temple. And he adds that the north side is the side of the body. Such a statement is incomprehensible to those who think rationally. Nonetheless such statements come from a very ancient knowledge and to dismiss them as 'old superstitions' is unintelligent. We can only lose something in the process.

What do we see happening? Gabriel announces to Zacharias the coming of John, and immediately after this his wife Elisabeth becomes pregnant. Gabriel announces the coming of Jesus to Mary, and immediately after this she becomes pregnant.

Moreover there is an old story which tells us of how Gabriel fetches the soul out of Paradise and instructs it for nine months while the body in which the soul is to live is growing in the mother's body.

In this way Gabriel is associated with the human body. We rational people think differently these days. We think that sperm meets ovum and that through a series of automatic processes a body starts to exist. This is very simplistic reasoning.

Imagine that you go to your work every day at eight o'clock and that you return home daily at six. Now next to you a house is being built by workmen who arrive at half-past-eight in the morning and go home at five. Thus you never see them. The only thing you see is that next to your house another one is growing and that one fine day it is finished without your ever having seen anyone working on it. And then you get new neighbours, and you visit them. Surely you are not going to say, 'I've watched your home grow day by day. Amazing, isn't it, the way such a thing grows all by itself!' They would think you were a little crazy. And yet we are all crazy in that way when we think that a child grows 'automatically' in its mother's body.

A new child is not like some magic Japanese flower which unfolds itself when you throw it into the amniotic fluid. That child was carefully constructed, even if you did not see the contractors.

110

But why is the side of the body connected with the north? In the old system of belief, the north meant danger! Many invasions of barbarian peoples came from the north. And then a number of things become much clearer. Moving into a body is a dangerous business. From the moment of conception we find ourselves in mortal danger. The equilibrium of our body is precarious, and every day is another day survived. We do not really notice much of this but our body is continually battling against all manner of threats. There is the primal power inside us which we see in the cells with their unbridled power for growth. If that is unleashed we have cancer. And then there is the primal power on the outside: the struggle for life. As well as the struggle against infections from bacteria, viruses and poisonous substances. These are two giants who stand face to face. And because they are equally strong it is quiet. But it is a conspicuous quietness. Should one of these forces fall away, then we are attacked by the other. When underfed, when the cells of our body have been left with only a little resistance, epidemics spread through humanity and tens of thousands are cut down from outside. If we live too luxuriously and if our cells grow too powerful, then cancer leaps on us from within and mows down tens of thousands. Living on this earth is a perilous existence. That is why we are told that when Gabriel fetched the soul from Paradise it protested vehemently. The soul knows that it is dangerous here on earth. That is why the name Gabriel as well as the word for man, is connected with the word hero.

But apart from the danger to our bodies, there are greater dangers down here. We can lose our souls and be unable to find the way home. Then we will have wandered far from Paradise but will not be going back. People in the olden days used to be familiar with the fear of losing their soul. Nowadays people do not even know they have a soul, so at least they have lost that anxiety.

As far as Gabriel is concerned we can say that we have all known him before we were born.

Do not think, 'How is this possible, with all those millions of people?' For in a world where time is different from that in our own, there are oceans of time in which to make personal contact with Gabriel without ever causing that good angel too much work. Perhaps the behaviour of the group of deep contemplatives was caused through their remembrance of Gabriel's instructions. Not that they remembered them consciously, but nonetheless they knew that there had been intense contact.

When we involve angels in our thoughts then a completely new attitude to life comes into existence. Then you do not say, 'What incredible luck!' on escaping from some accident. No, you say, 'Thank you, Lord for sending an angel on my path!' And you know that this body of ours, fragile and yet strong, is connected in some way to such an exalted ruler as Gabriel. Then you understand why our bodies are so much wiser than we are ourselves. If you listen carefully to your body you will come to know this. It warns us constantly, 'Watch it, this food is not suitable!' 'Remember, you must relax.'

There was a man, called McDougall, who contracted multiple sclerosis. He became lame and ended up in a wheelchair. Then McDougall's wife began to listen to the body of her husband. With endless patience she observed his reactions after every sort of food she gave him. After months of work she had worked out a diet which was specially suited to him. It is most moving to see photographs of McDougall which were taken a few years later. A friendly old man with white hair, a white waistcoat, a bow tie and coat with a fur collar, jumping up and down on one leg. Because it appeared that McDougall could not tolerate cereals he became so enthusiastic that he advised everyone with multiple sclerosis to go on a diet free from cereals. And although some people did benefit, others had no luck. And in Germany there was even a doctor called Evers who cured multiple sclerosis patients by using a lot of cereals. You cannot generalise when it comes to people. You must teach them to listen carefully to the wisdom of their own bodies. That is why the current tendency to give a limited number of universal medicines to one and all is such a dangerous one. If you apply totalitarian thinking to human bodies then you do not cure them. You kill them. Every person in turn is a separate creation with his own needs. People who think in a dictatorial way become irritated if they notice something of this. Hence, for instance, some strong attacks on homeopathic medicines. There are substances which must be prescribed on a very individual basis and that does not suit the totalitarian intellectuals that run the different national equivalents of the Department of Health and Welfare. These people would prefer to see all of us as completely identical, fitted with a number of slots and a number of little lamps. When the lamp above the headache slot lights up, give it a headache tablet. When the lamp above the anxiety slot lights up, some different medication.

Unfortunately, that is not how man is built. In a way, the man infected with the totalitarian virus is a much sicker man than the sick man for whom he makes the law.

Gabriel is different. He, on the contrary, respects the absolute individuality of each person. Perhaps the Creator left it to this angel to separately engrave with endless patience the fingerprints of each individual.

It is said that Gabriel not ony launches us into this world but also waits for us after death. He gives us cradle to grave security. How could a soul possibly lose its way after death? Well, it does not have to but in the course of this earthly life it can build up an antipathy to angels. And then it is possible to avoid even Gabriel.

Raziel

The name Raziel means 'God is my pleasure'.

This is an angel who has involved himself deeply with humanity in a positive and beneficial way.

It is told in the Hebrew tradition that when Adam, the first man, was driven from Paradise, he immediately encountered the problem of human illnesses. It would appear that it was the angel Raziel who gave Adam a book in which were set out all medicinal herbs in the world which could cure every possibly illness that might occur amongst mankind.

It seems to me to be important to realise that the medicine treasure chest of humanity is rarely found through the use of logical and analytical thought. More often it is discovered through intuition, as for instance in this century, Dr Bach discovered the thirty-eight flower remedies.[1] Bach did not discover these through experiment and logical discussion but simply through sitting for hours at a time in front of a flower and then he felt the symptoms welling up within himself against which the flower could help, such as holly for jealousy and hate, and willow for resentment. (Both are emotions which can lead to serious physical illnesses.)

There is an old saying that for every ill there is a cure, and when the doctor is at his wit's end he may say, 'There is no herb grown that will cure this disease.' If he is honest he will admit what he actually means is that he simply does not know the herb. For somewhere in the primeval forests, the very same which are being decimated with frightening rapidity by avaricious timber entrepreneurs, there are to be found whole legions of strong medicinal herbs which even show positive results with cancer.

1 *The Medical Discoveries of Edward Bach* by Nora Weeks published by The C. W. Daniel Company, Saffron Walden, Essex.

114

It is a beautiful thought that the angel Raziel actually gave Adam advice on how to deal with illnesses which had not yet come into existence. First the cure was created and only then does the illness that belongs to it come into existence. That is how we can see that curing and saving are the goals of creation, and not sickness and destruction. The emphasis is on love and happiness, not on disaster and hate.

Every person who finds pure and friendly means to rescue people from their maladies is inspired by the book of the angel Raziel. For the books of angels are not like the books of people. They are alive and present in the angelic heavens and he who is sensitive can read them.

Unfortunately these mild remedies are denounced more and more by the Dutch equivalent of Medicare; the technocratic bureaucracy demands scientific proof. A cure — however strange it may sound — is not proof. Twenty dead mice are proof. That is how mad we have all become nowadays.

The actual cure however, is not brought by the angel Raziel. Healing is associated with another great archangel.

Raphael

The name Raphael means 'God cures'. That is because he, like every self-respecting angel, refuses to take the credit. He is the force that is behind every cure. It is good to know that. In my medical career I have been amazed over and over again that a wound that has been stitched always seems to finish up as a neat line. You find yourself accidently saying out loud, 'Nicely stitched', within earshot of the patient. But in reality it is a great miracle that the wound closes up. You only realise this properly when something goes wrong and the stitches do not hold or if there develops what is called a kelloid, that is a thick scar grown proud of the surrounding skin. The structure is not repaired and we realise that the cure, even of something as apparently simple as a wound, is not in any way automatic.

More is needed than just sutures or some medicine. Every cure needs the help of heaven. They are not simply automatic processes. Automation exists only in the machines we have built ourselves.

In the Apocrypha we meet Raphael when he cures Tobias of blindness.

We really do need Raphael in this century, since the great spiritual blindness of people seems to be that we are taught to think that every process has some natural explanation. That every process, given some effort, could be understood by science.

That road is simply a cul-de-sac. We live in a world of wonders, even if they are well hidden, as for example in the closing up of a wound. Raphael has been clearly seen in this century by the English nurse Joy Snell. In the book she wrote which, since it first appeared in 1918, has been reprinted nine times, she tells us how she regularly sees a shining and cheerful angel at the heads of patients who are seriously ill. His right arm is raised, the forefinger pointing upwards, a gesture of hope. Every time she saw this figure she knew her patient would get better, and she often surprised the doctors with her accurate predictions.

Raphael has his own place in the Temple, and that is on the west side. This is the last part of the Temple, the holy of holies, the end of the road. Even as the sun goes up in the east and sets in the west, so the voyage of man is depicted symbolically as a voyage from east to west.

What wonders we see on this voyage of mankind! Even before his illnesses manifested themselves he was handed the herbs that could cure them. The voyage cannot in all truth be made without pain and sickness. The struggle is part of it all, but fortunately help is plentifully available.

And then at the end of the voyage we see the angel Raphael, symbol of the definitive cure. Help on the way here and redemption at the end. That is the truth about this voyage.

Compare if you like this optimistic vision with the false teachings of Karl Marx. He says that the path of humanity consists of generations who are 'fertiliser' spread on the fields of the future and that eventually a generation will arise who will live to enjoy the real communist paradise. A paradise that seems to recede further and further into the mists of the future as you approach nearer and nearer and that seems to be merely a pacifier for the people that live in the present and under bondage.

Karl Marx, Stalin, Lenin and their followers have fortunately been mistaken. Thank God that creation is put together in a better fashion. The Creator takes into account healing and the happiness of humanity over all times gone by. God's healing angel looks after the needs of everyone even in these days. Even the cure of a bout of flu', a scratch or a headache is somehow related to the great curative powers that flow through Raphael. Raphael is not someone who is distant and lived once long ago. He is an everyday-practical reality for those who have eyes and can see.

Metatron

The next very important personage in the heavens is the angel Metatron. His is a gigantic task. You could call him the head of the archives or the secretary of God, if we are to take descriptions of him seriously.

In connection with Metatron the Hebrew legends mention something extraordinary. They say that he was not always an angel but that at one time he was born on earth as a man. He was then called Hanoch, the seventh Patriarch counting from Adam. In the King James version of Genesis he is known as Enoch.

That he was special is immediately apparent from the announcement that he walked with God and was taken up by Him. According to this story therefore he did not die, the only other incidence of this we are given is the prophet Elijah.

Now to this mysterious figure is ascribed a book. It is the apocryphal book of Hanoch dating from the first century A.D. That it was recorded only then does not necessarily mean that it did not exist at an earlier date. It is said that in days of old people knew complete books by heart. That is still said also of Homer. These books were passed on literally for generations. Finally, when this ability lessened, people began hesitantly to write down the texts and that happened only in the couple of centuries prior to our Christian era.

That is when the book of Hanoch, or Enoch, also appeared. If someone has developed a real taste for angels, then he ought to read this book. They are mentioned in large numbers, and both their names and functions are set down. Even the fallen angels are not forgotten. It is extremely interesting to find that in the book some twenty-one fallen angel princes are named together with a precise description of what they actually do to corrupt humanity. Thus there is a fallen angel called Kasdeja who teaches people how they should commit abortions.

The most important thing we know about Metatron seems to me to be the fact just mentioned that he is the recording angel of God. Here we touch on the knowledge that all that happened is recorded. By means of hypnotism we have discovered that in our personal lives everything we have seen, done, spoken and experienced is registered literally, and that this registration starts at the moment of conception.

The text of Matthew 12, verse 36 which says that people must take into account on the day of reckoning each careless word they have spoken, appears — to use a suitable metaphor — technically quite feasible. You only need to press the 'play' button to listen to each spoken word. It must have seemed a strange idea to previous generations but for us with our tape and video recorders it is much more easily understood. After all, these types of inventions are only an externalisation of things which are with us.

You could say that in our creation there is a sort of double-entry bookkeeping system. Everything that happens here is recorded in archives over there, in the invisible world. That makes it a little easier for us to understand when, for instance, Swedenborg and Lorber say that whatever you do or say here on earth forms the framework of the surroundings in which you will find yourself after physical death.

A human being on earth is really to be regarded as a caterpillar, and his death as the chrysalis. Out of this comes either a heavenly Red Admiral or a Death's Head Moth, an inhabitant of heaven or of hell.

It is all like that children's game of Oranges and Lemons. I remember as if it were yesterday how one rushed through under all those arms and was caught by the chopper and then came the whispered question, 'Oranges or lemons?'

Well, that is when you ended up on either the left side or the right side, and eventually there was a tug o'war and that is exactly what the Bible says: you belong to either the sheep or the goats (Matthew 25, verse 32) and that is exactly what Swedenborg says: you end up in either a hellish or heavenly company.

Heaven and hell are populated from this earth and so they hold each other in balance. Two enormous spiritual powers are balanced, but because they are balanced you notice nothing. But if you add a feather to the left or to the right side, then the whole load starts moving. That is why an apparently insignificant decision can have such an enormous effect.

As far as Swedenborg is concerned, after you have been assigned to a heavenly or a hellish company the file is closed. Another famous visionary from the last century, Lorber, makes some more additions in his extensive series of books. He is of the opinion that, however deep a person has sunk, there are still chances for almost everyone, even if only after much time has passed. (Though it seems curious to speak of the passing of time in a timeless region.)

Lorber is thus seen to be nearer to the apocryphal evangelism of St Paul that I mentioned while telling the story of Michael.

In any case, the sins and good deeds of commission and omission are 'recorded' and that recording influences one's future lot. And Metatron is the angel who supervises these books.

There are more archangels than those I have named. Traditionally there are seven. Both Jewish and Christian thinkers have busied themselves intensively with this subject over the last few thousand years.

I only wanted to tell you about a few of these archangels, and I hereby offer my apologies to the angels I have not mentioned. They will not hold it against me since their only desire is to indicate the almighty power and magnificence of the God who has created all with His word.

120

Let us once more take a look at the three groups of angels we have discussed. The princes and the archangels next to each other, the guardian angels nearest to man.

Archangels Angel princes	} Formative world
Guardian angels	
Man	} Material world

Angel princes rule over complete nations but sometimes they go even further. The culture of one nation then rules over part of the world for a very long time, as for instance the way ancient Rome set the tone for Europe for many centuries. Then possibly an angel prince becomes temporarily the chairman of an assembly.

Dionysius called such assemblies 'choirs'. These choirs have as their purpose the praising of the Lord. Praising the Lord can be done through other means than singing a psalm. Every action by which a town, a region or a country works towards a cleaner, better and friendlier earth, is a hymn of praise.

Who does not remember the great disaster of London in the 1950s, when a few thousand people choked on the infamous smog, the mixture of fog and soot and exhaust fumes. Then London changed over to smokeless fuel and the era of smog passed. I believe that such a measure is a hymn of praise.

Every person who, whether at national, provincial or even municipal level, sets a policy through which more tolerance, more friendliness, more beauty and more purity become the norm, can be sure that he is invisibly supported and inspired by angel choirs whose channel of communication he forms at that moment.

You will notice in my diagram how the guardian angels stand near the border between the lowest heaven and earth.

And there are other things below man. These are the dark world of chaos and hate, the 'hells'. We can continually choose between inspiration from heaven or from hell. The only thing we cannot choose is neutrality. Our soul is provided with a switch having only two positions — either up or down.

There is a beautiful story about the difference between heaven and hell. Once there was a man who asked an angel about that difference, and the angel said, 'Come with me.'

First they came to hell, and there you saw a number of people sitting at a tremendously long table on which stood the most incredibly delicious dishes, but the people could not flex their arms at the elbow so they could not bring the food to their mouths. Their arms were also so long that there was no possibility of taking in any food. There they sat. They looked at the food hungrily and suffered the pangs of starvation.

Then the angel took the man to heaven, and there he saw precisely the same set-up. Delicious food and people with inflexible long arms. Only these were enjoying the food because everyone fed the person sitting directly opposite them.

To return to the subject of angels: It seems quite important to me that we should take seriously the possibility that angels are much more closely related to us than is normally thought. If they really have experienced a stage of being human, as is thought by Swedenborg as well as Rudolf Steiner — the founder of anthroposophy — then they are of a kind that is similar to us. Then we observe how God created beings in a timeless spiritual realm, how these beings went on to endure circulation through time, after which they are born as a good spirit (angel) or a bad spirit (devil). And the third possibility is that you have to do your homework once more till you get it right.

Whatever the case may be, I hope you have a good laugh the next time you see the Party leaders of the Kremlin reviewing a May the first parade, or in recent history Bokassa placing the imperial crown on his own head. You will then realise that you are looking at film extras and that the real leaders are sitting elsewhere.

Ouspensky says that the higher a person is placed the less freedom of action he has. The least liberated is the sole ruler for he is totally determined by the destiny of his people, a destiny that is not in his hands but in the forces which pull the invisible strings. Perhaps that is why autocrats make those wooden puppet-like gestures. And it is also just as well to know that the ordinary citizen is the man with the greatest freedom. And that, if he uses his freedom to improve the lot of his fellow-men, he will get unexpected help. Personal help from his guardian angel and a higher form of aid from the angel ruler who can gather together the intentions of many well-meaning people in a miraculous way and weave them into the destiny of a whole nation.

It is remarkable how many free citizens are busy once more to improve the whole environment using small-scale methods. They run circles round the bureaucracies and get on with it. They grow organic vegetables and the mighty factories with their artificial fertilisers and their poisonous sprays grit they teeth as they look on.

They demand homoeopathic remedies and the pharmaceutical industry does its best to limit this alternative via extensive lobbying of the relevant government agencies.

They try to interest people in wind energy, solar energy. They march en masse against deadly atomic energy. Something is happening. A ground swell seems to be arising from below, which is trying to wash away pollution of the environment.

Unfortunately there is another team. These are the ones who do not care what happens to others. They are the ones who force others to smoke along 'passively' in offices, so that the non-smoker also gets lung cancer. They are the ones who pollute the world with noise and who do not seem to have any real social awareness.

Which group is the stronger?

There is no way we can tell but the angel ruler of a nation can correlate the inner reality of a whole nation and that is how the destiny of a nation is formed. In this way every citizen on the street of every nation is directly responsible for the government that that nation gets. It may look like the result of an election or of the setting up of a dictatorship but that is not so. There exists a detour via heaven. If there are not enough people who take a real interest in their environment, the government will turn a blind eye to pollution and thus open wide the door to many illnesses. We must, of course, make allowances when discussing all this, for the difference in 'real time' between heaven and earth, whereby the indifference of yesterday is the cause of the unpleasantness of today. And that 'yesterday' can well lie some decades in the past.

The action that you undertook today against the people amongst whom you are living, comes back via a celestial 'computer' to earth some decades later. Never think that what you do is unimportant, when you are taking on the big batallions.

It is precisely you, the little citizen, who can take on the oppressive bureaucracy and tilt it from its high horse, if only you have the right attitude. The dictator who will not take over in twenty years time stays away because you took the righty decision today.

You are more important than you think!

4. Two Higher Heavens

A. The Creative World

We usually talk — that is if we talk about it at all — simply about heaven and earth. Ancient tradition, however, knew several heavens, the one higher or lower than the next.

In the previous chapter we talked about the first heaven, the 'formative' one. We will now deal with the second one, which is called the heaven of creation. If the earth is likened to a cake and the formative heaven is the cake tin then the second heaven is the place where the cake is baked, that is the bakery.

Despite its name, the Creation did not come from this heaven. It would be better to think of this heaven as being the place where the pure realm of creative ideas is transformed into the more closely-knit region of forces and fields which knead and form our own visible world. The second heaven is a mediating region.

And once again, in this second heaven we come across angel hierarchies. In the system of Dionysius they are given beautiful names such as exousiai, dunamis and kuriotetes. These words are translated as powers (or authorities), forces and dominions. Remarkable names and ones which at first sight may not be easily understood.

Do not imagine fearsome monsters with scales and antennae; instead imagine angels in human form but tremendously bright.

Let us begin with the exousiai, the powers. In Romans 13, verse 1 it says that the soul must be subject to the powers.

9 Our own Milky Way is part of a much larger whole, the family of galaxies. This is a photograph of one. It is an image of the third heaven which encompasses the second and the first

This is an important point. They are thus seen to be placed over our souls, so that they stand, as it were, one storey higher than the guardian angels in the territory of the first heaven. Guardian angels quite often come to the aid of our bodies when these are in a perilous situation. The exousiai have their area of work in the deeper regions of our soul. We cannot therefore meet them without further ado in this earthly abode. Perhaps we meet them in visions and dreams. Perhaps they are related to the archetypes, those mighty forces discovered by Jung and which can express themselves in our souls.

I must now talk about a certain concept without which it will not be clear to you how it is that I can determine the exact position of all these angel hierarchies with so much accuracy. Imagine that you are looking at a street map of London. A maze of streets and squares and the Thames running right across it all. Now take a transparent plastic map. This is exactly the same size as the street map and on the plastic is drawn the whole network of subway trains. When you superimpose this plastic map exactly over the London street map, suddenly the underground stations and their connecting tracks appear. You then have an idea of how to get quickly from one side of the city to the other and precisely which line you must take.

Well now, it may sound strange, but a similar map has been passed on to us from very ancient times. It is a type of plastic overlay that you can lay onto an existing set of facts so that places and connections that were at first obscure, suddenly seem to stand out.

Let us take an example. We all know the Ten Commandments. These have been given us in that order, and there they stand. One does not seem of more importance than the next. But if you take this model of which I was speaking just now, and lay it over the Ten Commandments then something else happens. Then you see the first three commandments arranged in a triangle with the apex pointing upwards. That the second and third series of three commandments each lie immediately below the first, and that their peaks point downwards. And that the last commandment, the tenth one, takes a lonely position at the foot of it all.

You can see also, on this very ancient model, that there are special connections between all the commandments and that every commandment has a special colour, a special character. Just as the London Underground map uses different colours for the Central Line, the Circle Line, the District Line etc.

Everywhere that we meet with ten or nine or even seven components in the Creation or in ancient writings we can use this ancient model. We can superimpose it on the series and determine the character of each point and examine the connections.

Take your time and imagine a transparent sheet of plastic, with three triangles drawn on it, one below the other; the peak of the first triangle pointing upwards and the other two pointing down, and finally, right at the foot, one more point. Each of the ten positions of this composite figure has a particular name and a particular characteristic. The first one is called the 'crown' and thus if we come across a series of ten in the Creation or in ancient writings we then know that the first one of that series has a 'crown' character. From this position it is possible to say something about what really dominates the whole series of ten. Or if you look at the sixth position you will know that every sixth position in such a series of ten is connected with the creation of harmony.

To our logical Western way of thinking these are almost incomprehensible matters, even if modern physics is beginning to come close to this strange way of composite thought.

Footnote

I refer those who want to know more about the celestial map to one of the books written about the ten Sephiroth.

The word is derived from the Hebrew word meaning 'to count' or 'to tell (a story)'. The ten Sephiroth tell us about the ten focuses of the Creation.

We can now return to our nine hierarchies. If you lay the ancient chart, the 'Underground' map, over this, you suddenly see that the hierarchies do not simply lie in a neat single line running from top to bottom but that they lie in three groups of three. First a series of three with one at the top and the other two to the left and right immediately beneath. Then, as in a sort of mirror image, two more to the left and right next to each other with the third vertex of the triangle a little below. Then, below this, another threesome arranged in the same way. Finally a single one beneath it all, a loner.

And just as our plastic map of the underground has indications such as Piccadilly Circus, Hammersmith and Baker Street, so the nine hierarchies of Dionysius can be identified such as harmony, power, foundation and so forth.

This way of reasoning is of course not scientifically defensible but in fact we are not talking about nature but about the heavens, and there the laws of symbols and analogies rule, and not the laws of logic and derivative analysis.

According to this diagram we are now able to place the powers (or exousiai). Compare the classification with that of our planet. You have areas which you could call rugged and other ones that have a grandeur about them, such as the Alps. Some are lovely or friendly such as Somerset or Exmoor. Yet others are fresh, such as the Frisian-lakes country.

The heavens are classified in the same way; not by a name such as Piccadilly Circus or a description such as 'rugged', but instead according to an internal quality. I have referred to it already using names such as 'harmony' and 'force'.

The Powers 'live' in the area called 'harmony'. It is that part of the second heaven which borders the first heaven. They are the border people between the second and first heavens, just as the guardian angels dwell on the border between the first heaven and the earth.

The task of the Powers inhabiting the region of 'harmony' is the reconciliation of opposites. And that is also the precise reason why they have been put in charge of our souls. For our souls are the territory where the great struggle is fought. Our souls are not a unity. They consist of pairs of opposites that appear to us as paradoxes. Good and evil, love and hate, sympathy and antipathy, joy and sorrow. Often man chooses one and rejects the other. And then he sees with terror that the more he chooses one quality, the more the other comes rushing in. The restless seeker after pleasure is faced with sorrow. Passionate love can turn unexpectedly into hate. The person with good intentions can perpetrate great evil.

And yet we must choose, and certainly between good and evil, and between love and hate. How is a person to resolve that paradox? Must he say, 'I might as well do wrong since good will come out of it anyway?' Or must he say, 'I will not choose the good since I will be only calling up evil?' These are wrong solutions. Man must choose and know at the same time that contradiction is present.

If you pull out of the struggle you will fall victim to the spirits of confusion who will break you into small pieces. You then become a tough executive in the office and a devout Christian in church.

No, we must choose in this great paradoxical world of our soul and we must not be afraid if we are confronted with the opposite. Just as a farmer must not be afraid when weeds grow in his fields. If we consciously choose the positive and the good then, although the opposite force will appear, the Powers will also come to help and they will interweave the contradictions so as to form a higher unity. Then even the things that annoy you in your loved ones take on something mellowing. Then it is as if even the evil for which you have been forgiven has helped to make a milder person of you.

As soon as you are dealing with heaven you start seeing paradoxes. The narrow vision of physics would try to force us to see the world from only one single aspect of the Creation. Thus we still do not consider that anything not scientifically proved has any right to exist. This is a tremendous trap into which we must not fall. I cannot prove scientifically that I love someone and yet it is of enormous importance in my life. I can prove scientifically that my love weighs 120 pounds but that is not really important to me (although it may be to her).

No, the real things that matter in this life can be stated only in terms of paradox. Only if something is both yes and no is it real and true. And that is the business of the Powers. They interweave light and darkness into masterpieces, just as Rembrandt did.

They are concerned with yet more matters. The reconciliation of paradoxes also means making peace, yet another paradox. The call for peace has never been so strong as in this century, the chance for peace never so small. Perhaps peace is a matter of arithmetic.

It may be that when there is enough peace within enough souls, war will keep its distance. However, if there is a lot of discord in a lot of souls, then the eventual outcome will be war, in the real world.

If that is so, then it is of the utmost importance that we dedicate ourselves to peace within our souls and the resolution of paradoxes, however maddeningly difficult that last can be. And we will often be asked to resolve these internal contradictions through problems set by the outer world.

Take the simple case of someone who wants to tell the truth at all times and who is forced to lie, of which we saw many examples during the war. At that time lives would have been lost if the truth had been told to the occupation forces.

Or take the case of a woman who has always sought out the beautiful and whose breast must be amputated.

Or the case of a refined and gentle person who sees a friend beaten to death in a concentration camp.

What happens inside these souls? What kind of storm rages within? How do they come through it all?

In addition there are many problems which are insoluble. It takes a long time before you realise this, but nonetheless it is so. A wise man once remarked that if a problem has no solution then it is no longer a problem but a fact of life. A fact of life which you must just bear in mind the way you do a curve in the road.

But the problem hurts you just as much. And yet, if you continue to trust, help will come. Then the Powers are told by a greater authority to help us and then serenity flows through our souls. Then the mood is changed from mild depression to tempered optimism.

Those who try to make peace get help, even if they do not succeed in realising this ideal in the real world. They are changed from within.

You can pick these people out, if only by their radiance. Just as you can pick out the ones who have the opposite attitude. Actually, I believe that the opposite of peace is not so much war as dissatisfaction. Make a point of noticing how many mouths are forever pulled down at the corners. How many faces have hardened into perpetual disapproval. How many eyes show themselves as eternally wronged. I am afraid it is that which will eventually bring on a war.

Of course, there are real matters which can cause us to be dissatisfied, but nowadays great delight is taken in the creation of dissatisfaction. And I am afraid that when discontent has reached its peak, the outside world will answer obediently and allow us to see war. Then there will be true reason for dissatisfaction, but by then it will be too late.

Is every war really caused by dissatisfaction? Fundamentally, yes.

If Hitler had been contented with just Germany or Napoleon with just France or sixteenth-century Spain with just Spain or Caesar with just Italy, etc., then we would have seen few wars. But all those leaders and their wretched companions wanted more and yet more and they always found people who were dissatisfied with their piece of land or their humble position on earth and who wanted to march along with them.

In my opinion, the most terrifying part of this second half of the twentieth century is that this disaffection is not limited to the upper crust but has become something common to us all. These days it is almost a sign of deviance if you say you are happy in your work and with your family.

This cultivated discontent is what can cause dangerous tensions to build up but if we realise that, a possible war can be avoided — if enough people change their internal attitudes through being satisfied and making peace within their own small circle. And exactly at the point where we start making peace, the Powers come to our aid. One of these seems powerful enough to me to hold back a complete army, but they only do that if they have enough friends here on earth. For angels need people in order to intervene here on earth.

If I make peace I will have made a channel through which the Powers can descend onto this earthly vale. I say through deliberately, for again the Powers only borrow their might.

If I disturb the peace then I close this channel and then the disintegrating forces automatically start their work, just as the body starts to disintegrate as soon as the soul has departed.

From the position of these mighty angels of peace in the creative heavens, that is the heavens where active new creations manifest themselves, it appears that every peace is in fact a form of creation.

In politics it is often thought that peace these days is kept through the balance of terror. Enough cruise missiles on each side of the line, but that is not true. The peace that results is at the most an uneasy truce.

We see two power-blocs confronting each other, and the fact that nobody has as yet dared to press the button is called peace. Nonsense. Neither the one, nor the other power-bloc keeps the peace in this manner. The only one who gains from it all is the armaments industry.

When I speak about two superpowers keeping a balance of terror I realise quite well that the rearmament of the U.S.A. is a direct result of the gigantic war-effort of the Soviet Union. I also realise that the communists have repeatedly and openly announced that eventually they will rule the world. I understand that what is happening at the moment is a logical and realistic build-up of arms. Almost like a mathematical solution.

And yet I believe that ultimately this will not bring peace. No, peace itself is an active third force. A force that cannot come forth from the opposing power-blocs. The creation of real peace is thus always something original. Something unexpected. Something new. Often so strange that you just have to laugh.

Perhaps both power-blocs will be unexpectedly dismantled from within because on both side of the Iron Curtain there will be enough young people who show their enthusiasm for solar and wind energy. If enough energy is raised that is dependent on neither the state nor the multi-nationals, then you achieve an enormous decentralisation of power. Then, in the long run, it becomes impossible for any authority to get the soldiers marching. I merely mention one original possibility which could result in a peaceful influence external to the power structure. We have seen those unexpected solutions before.

Take the solitary ruler and his absolutely subservient people. If things really got too bad, the king was murdered and then the liberator became sole ruler and the whole problem started over again. From arbitrariness to murder and revolution and then again back to arbitrariness.

And then in England was found a rather strange solution: the constitutional monarchy. This did not depose the sole ruler and replace him with another, but it removed his power. He is then tamed, and from being a mighty tyrant became a friendly centre point.

Not that this always succeeded at first, but in the long run the formula became a success and it still works. Much better than any dictatorship.

I said that the translation of the word exousiai could be 'power'. And with this an interesting light is thrown on the idea of power as it exists in heaven.

Authorities are, according to heaven, those who have the power to create harmony out of contradictions. They are nearer to poets than to rulers. And man is asked to subject his soul to these powers.

Someone who keeps the peace in his country by torturing his opponents in psychiatric institutions is seen by heaven as a disaster and not as an authority, while someone who is aware from his high position that he is a servant of the people and continually tries to find original ways of resolving contradictions is seen by heaven as a real authority.

In the second heaven, as we mentioned earlier, two further choirs of angels are to be found, namely the kuriotetes (Dominions) and dunamis (Virtues). Try asking a person for his definition of the word 'dominion'.

There is a strong possibility that he or she will start using words such as command, police, arrogance, slavery etc. Unfortunately the word dominion has become charged with all these negative connotations.

In heaven it is totally different. If I take the ten-fold symbol and lay it over the nine choirs of angels, then I see the Dominions living in a region that is indicated by the word 'mercy'. That is strange because dominion and mercy rarely go together in this world. Rulers can show mercy if they get out of bed on the right side that morning, but since they seldom do so, mercy seems to be a rarity in this century.

Heaven, however, dominates by love and not by the whip. Thus the Dominions are channels of mercy. Channels, no more and no less.

In the economy of the soul, mercy is of tremendous importance. I recently heard a lecture by Ian Pearce, the man who is the proponent in England of what is known as the Simonton method of treatment for cancer patients. He tells a number of moving stories about patients who have contracted cancer after they had been unable to forgive either something done to them or something they had done to another. The hatred for the unforgiven person or the guilt they felt for the mistake they had made and for which they had not forgiven themselves was enough to start the development of a cancer that proved fatal to them.

Or, and that gave a lot of hope, when these people forgave either themselves or the other person, then you sometimes saw how the progress of the sickness was halted and a real cure became possible.

Pearce said, 'Resentment which is not released and guilt which is not forgiven are two of the most destructive forces in the world.' And by 'destructive' he really means what he says when he talks about the body being literally destroyed.

We must therefore think of mercy and forgiveness when we visit that part of heaven where the exalted Dominions live. Forgiveness and mercy, are, as much creative concepts as harmony and peace. It is a sobering thought that mercy is one of the basic concepts of the Creation. It is reconciliation and mercy rather than oxygen or carbon atoms which are the building blocks of Creation. Everyone who neglects to take this into account clashes with the laws that maintain the universe. Merciless dictatorships — whether these are of the left or of the right — are a real symptom of degeneration. They stay on for a time as rulers because dirt floats on the surface for a while before it sinks away, but they have in fact long since sawn off the branch on which they sit. Their eventual disappearance is assured.

But people and states that have taken forgiveness into their own lives and into their codes of law can rule over the hearts of their opponents and can be assured of the continued help of the mighty Dominions.

Do not imagine that the Dominions intervene forcefully if there is no mercy. Something much worse happens. They do nothing.

Beneath the nine choirs of angels are to be found nine other choirs — or screechers, rather than choirs. These are the spirits of darkness and confusion. If the Dominions cannot find room somewhere in a country's constitution, then the analogous hellish hierarchy takes over in that country, and hellish hierarchies do intervene.

They are simply champing at the bit to rule. They then go and teach such a nation how to build concentration camps and how to elevate mercilessness to a national virtue. Heaven never forces, but those who do not follow its will are sooner or later forced by hell.

A third angel hierarchy, called the dunamis or Virtues, lives in the creative heaven.

Now we must visit a totally different region of heaven. We leave the flowery meadows of the Dominions and the magnificent cornfields of the Powers and we come now to a rugged mountainous landscape, with sharp peaks and inhospitable glaciers.

What kind of angels are these? It is said of this hierarchy

that they 'remove obstacles'. And that is a great blessing because there are times when a person, whether he wants to or not, must stand up for himself.

There come times when his country is under occupation and he can no longer tolerate injustice, and so he goes underground. He lives in a bureaucratically-run state and runs into a brick wall because there seems to be no other way. The injustice, the indifference of officialdom, the arrogance of the high and mighty, it all becomes too much. People start fighting a losing battle for a just cause. For the preservation of a piece of forest. Against the building of an atomic power station. Against the culling of seals. Against the dumping of radio-active waste into the ocean. Against the fluoridation of the water supplies. Against all those things that make a dung-heap out of our world. In most cases those in power seem to win, that is the characteristic of power.

Yet that fight is not for nothing. Something seems to penetrate into people's heads. Others take over the torch and suddenly the lost cause appears to have won for once because the giant seems to have stumbled over his own feet for some incomprehensible reason. Just when you think, 'I just can't go on any more' the wind changes. The energy required to go on fighting flows towards you and you seem also to obtain more power from within. This is what is called 'getting your second wind'.

Beware that this extra supply of power is not a coincidence. That the man who really fights for a just cause has mightly allies. Combative angels who stand in the breach. Naturally they never do so without God's expressed will, but are always prepared to be near the lonely fighter in order to clear the course of obstacles.

But there is another side to the Virtues. How shall I explain? That is the fight against God Himself. That is the tragic extreme that can happen to man from time to time.

138

I once found a very devout friend of mind in a deep cloud of depression. It was as if her love for the Lord was at a very low ebb.

After I had probed a little, she came out with, 'There is something that I cannot reconcile, and to which God will not give an answer. Usually I can forget it for a time, but every now and then it returns and then I think, "how can you have permitted this?" '

I asked, 'Is it some particular event which you have in mind?'

'Yes,' she said. 'I visited the former concentration camp of Auschwitz. I saw a large room filled to the ceiling with the shoes of children who had been gassed. How can such a thing happen? However can a God who is love allow such a thing?'

Even she, who had been through so much in her lifetime, struggled with this problem.

Then there is the little Vietnamese child who runs up to an American soldier holding the arm that has been torn off in her remaining hand. And the pale little girl who sits sadly in her wheelchair during the healing service conducted by Kathryn Kuhlman, while an old man jumps up triumphantly from his wheelchair, the worn-out hip completely cured. (Kathryn was so angry with God about this seemingly misplaced healing that her friend Corrie ten Boom had to get up in the middle of the night to minister to her. This happened during a conference of the Holy Spirit in Jerusalem on March 3, 1974.) There is the mother who loses her only son to leukaemia just when he gets his first job, while the ninety-year-old senile grandfather lives on in a rest home.

You can try to explain these matters rationally. You can say that we ourselves do not stick to the rules, so what do we expect? Or we can look for the solution in concepts like Karma or reincarnation. Or we can decide that those children are much happier in heaven than down here. But that is avoiding the issue.

If we add it all up we find that there is a side to God that comes over as unjust, irrational and even cruel, and into which we run as if into a brick wall. And there is then a voice which whispers, 'That these things are permitted proves that there is no God, or that if He exists he is not worthy of being worshipped.'

Many people have fallen into this trap. It is the one inside you that impairs you, and who is a thousand times more dangerous than anyone who hinders from the outside. The outsider who interferes can at the most destroy your body, but the one inside who hinders may try to corrupt your soul.

Job struggled with that problem and people in our time are again striving against the same difficulty. Let me say that God does not mind if you struggle with Him. That eventually you raise your fist to heaven and say, 'Why is that allowed?' The man who then fights on, who does not give up, who asks and asks and, I would almost say whines, who takes God seriously — that man sometimes grows internally. Not that the problem is solved. The children's shoes remain in Auschwitz, the Vietnamese girl will go through life with only one arm, but it is just as if you have been lifted over and across the obstacle.

God distracted Job's attention. He did not say, 'You are quite right, Job, I have gone too far this time.' but He said, 'Knowest thou the time when the wild goats of the rock bring forth?'

What a strange answer. It reminds me of an experience I once had. I was with my two sons in the mountains and suddenly the eldest said, 'Daddy, are there any chamoix around?'

I peered at a low rock wall and said, 'Well, I think maybe they are behind there.'

'Come on, let's look,' he said, and before I knew what was going on I found myself panting and running behind the two boys. First over a mountain meadow and then straight up against the thirty foot high cliff. When I had climbed about twenty feet my boys suddenly disappeared over the top. I looked down and did not dare to move. I hung there sweating with an acute attack of vertigo and saw everything spinning. Suddenly the head of my eldest appeared over the edge and he said, 'What are you doing?'

Cursing my stupidity I climbed upwards with the courage of despair and let myself flop on the ground. Just there was a steep slope made up of stones that ended in a high cliff that towered some hundreds of feet above us and cast a deep shadow. And suddenly, not fifty feet from us a chamoix sprang up. The beast galloped straight at an enormous cliff and jumped onto an almost invisible ledge and trotted off to the left, appearing to be almost glued to the cliff, and disappeared before our astonished eyes.

'That,' I said, 'that was a chamoix.'

My sons had expected nothing less, they were at that delightful age when they had not started doubting my word.

I only wanted to tell this tale so as to make clear that I lost my fear of heights the moment I was caught in the beauty, the elegance and the power of the chamoix. I knew very well that I had to descend again, but that terrifying emptiness under my feet was now forgotten.

So it is with the man who wrestles with God. You are caught up in an overpowering fear of heights. Who is that God who allows this? And then suddenly He expands your awareness all around. The cliff is not gone, the abyss still gapes, but what does it matter — a beautiful chamoix runs in front of me. He who has given such an animal the power to effortlessly surmount such a rock face, should He not be able to bring everything under control, even if we do not see it down here?

The Virtues associate themselves with those who struggle. You notice then that you have many more invisible allies than you would have thought. Then the false inspirations are silenced.

I must add something to this exposition of the Powers, Dominions and Virtues.

In the course of history people have, a number of times, taken the angel hierarchies to be the actual creators of our visible world. One of the latest representatives of this school of thought was the anthroposophist, Rudolf Steiner. Steiner sees the Powers as those who create form and the Virtues as those who get things moving, as, for instance, from seed to full-grown plant, and the Dominions as those who bring wisdom to the plant. As instanced in the movement of a sunflower that follows the sun so as to catch the maximum amount of sunshine.

I mention this opinion for the sake of completeness, but I would like to add that I do not share it.

All angels, from the highest to the lowest, look up to their Creator and the most they can do is transmit. They are not creators but the created, just as we are.

When John receives the Revelation and throws himself at the feet of the mighty angel, he is told, 'Do not do that. I am thy fellow servant and of thy brethren that have the testimony of Jesus: worship God!' (Revelation 19, verse 10)

I think we would do well to take these words to heart.

And so we see that a new triangle is added to that of the first heaven.

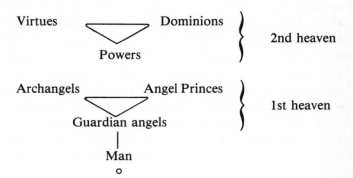

But we have not finished yet, for above the second heaven stretches a third, still deeper, greater and more tremendous than the second.

If you are not afraid of heights we will now start climbing up there.

B. The World in God's Shadow

There is a world that is so saturated with the glow of God's love that we who live on this distant and rather cold planet are almost unable to imagine such a place. And even in this world angels live.

Again I want to set up an angel triangle, but this time with the peak pointing upwards.

Seraphim

We begin with the uppermost vertex and place there the seraphim, the angels of love. That is the highest angel group. Let me warn you immediately that this word love has to be properly seen and understood. Over the last few decades love has come to mean almost all things to all men. To make love is to go to bed together. The love between two stars of the screen has passed in a single year and is transmuted into two other loves. 'I can't give you anything but love, baby,' as a well-known American singer sang. All those bumper-stickers with 'I love NY' etc. That is not what I am talking about. By love is meant the selfless love, which denies the self. Giving without expecting anything in return. The Greeks called it *agape*.

From this highest point of this highest world starts the Creation of heaven and earth. You must fully realise that the real essence of our whole Creation is love. If we should start searching beyond the hydrogen atom, the electron, and past the light quanta, then we would first find pure vibration. And if we were to look beyond these vibrations then we would discover that they are thoughts. And if we found that they were thoughts, then we would find warmth in them. These are not cool intellectual thoughts but warm thoughts.

And if we were to further investigate that warmth, then we would find it to be pure, giving love. And if we were to examine that love even more closely, we would eventually come to Him who gives that love. That is why it is said that the physically created, and the creations of the spirit, are stamped with the secret name of God Himself.

The prophet Isaiah tells that he saw the Lord sitting on a throne, high and lifted up (Isaiah 6, verse 1) and then he saw that the seraphim, the flaming angels were above it. Each of these angels had six wings: two covered his face, two his feet and two were used for flying.

What kind of mysterious announcement is this? It seems quite clear to me that something special is meant by those six wings. A whole series of abilities that can hardly be comprehended here on earth. To the best of my knowledge there is no animal with six wings, although a fossilized insect with six wings has been found. However, we must be especially careful to stop ourselves from viewing the six wings merely as a biological curiosity.

We have already spoken of the wings of angels as being a symbol of their ability to turn some unknown corner and thus appear in, and disappear from, our world. The well-known analogy that is used to clarify this is that of the Flatlanders. These are imaginary creatures dreamed up to explain how it must be to live in a world where height, the third dimension, does not exist. My pen, for instance, which comes all of a sudden from above to touch the paper, is a wonder for the Flatlanders. Letters appearing suddenly, out of the blue, from the third dimension.

So it is with the fourth dimension. We cannot see this one, and from that four-dimensional world an angel steps into our world. It is a miracle. The two wings indicate the angelic powers to do this. He can turn the corner.

But if we call the first heaven four-dimensional, then we could say that the second heaven is provided with a fifth dimension. To get from the first to the second heaven, a second set of wings is needed. And although we have never done so, we could picture the Dominions with four wings.

The third heaven has yet another dimension added, and becomes the world of six dimensions. Another pair of wings is necessary. Perhaps that is the reason why seraphim are depicted with six wings. With the pair covering his feet he can stride across the border between the earth and the first heaven. With the pair that is used for flying he can stride across the border between the first and second heavens, and with the pair that is used to cover his face he can finally stride across the border into the third heaven, the tremendous world of flight close by God. The seraph is at home in all worlds. Love knows no boundaries. (I have borrowed the idea of a sixth dimension from Ouspensky's 'A New Model of the Universe'.)

To my way of thinking, these exalted beings have a very boring task. They perpetually call out to each other, 'Holy, holy, holy is the Lord of Hosts, the whole earth is full of His glory.' Isaiah adds to this that the 'posts of the door moved at the voice of him that cried'.

Let us go together through a little exercise. I would like us both to listen to the call of the seraphim. 'Holy, holy, holy' is heard endlessly. But now you must listen to the Hebrew words, 'Kadosh, kadosh, kadosh.'

If you take the old Askenasi pronunciation, which is much closer to the original, it sounds like 'Kadoosh, kadoosh, kadoosh.'

What do you hear? Repeat it softly and slowly to yourself. Do you hear what I hear? Now do you understand why the posts of the door shook?

'Kadoosh, kadoosh, kadoosh.'

You hear the surf!

And precisely at this point I take a little excursion to that earth which finds itself in the middle of the energy crisis.

In 1857, in Yugoslavia, one of the greatest geniuses of this technical age, Nicola Tesla, was born. He later emigrated to America and worked with Edison. He discovered what are now known as Tesla currents.

Hans Nieper, in his book 'Revolution', tells us the story of how Tesla built a new kind of engine into his car. This used a six-foot aerial to draw energy 'from the ether'. The car drove at ninety miles an hour, never needed gasoline and was completely clean.

Tesla took the secret of his car to his grave, and all this happened in 1931.

What kind of energy was that?

That brilliant contemporary of Freud, Wilhelm Reich, had also discovered a new form of energy that he called 'orgone energy'. He found a way of collecting this energy and of using it for a variety of purposes, amongst other things, for curing cancer patients. He was also able, during a prolonged period of drought, to so direct this energy that rain fell. And according to his wife, Ilse, he was also able to run an engine on this form of energy. That happened in the nineteen-fifties.

You should consider Tesla and Reich as a sort of run-up to the man I really want to talk about now — T. Henry Moray. His book, 'The Sea of Energy in which the Earth Floats' has just been reprinted through the efforts of his sons.

Moray was an electrical engineer who said that the cosmos contained enough energy to allow everyone on earth to switch on one and half million 100 watt lamps. Was this American exaggeration?

In 1911 Moray said that a gigantic energy field reaches the earth in waves, just as waves of the sea pound the beach. He called this energy 'Radiant Energy' and indeed he was able to use it to power a 100 watt bulb. He used a long aerial and an earth, but no other source of energy in his demonstration to many people.

In 1937 he switched on forty light bulbs of 100 watts. A photograph of this event is shown in his book.

Moray's bulbs burned with a very special clear light, a sort of daylight. His apparatus, not much bigger than a suitcase, never even became warm. And if you did not switch it off it just went on delivering energy. The only difficulty encountered when switching on was that you had to search for the field. You had to tune in as with a radio station. As well as the fact that no heat was generated, there was also no sound.

Moray said that the apparatus was nothing but a cosmic energy pump.

It transformed the onrushing energy waves into direct current. More or less in the way our heart does with its valves which are arranged so that the blood can flow in only one direction. Or in the way that if you allowed the first wave of a series of waves that rushed in from the sea to fill a basin and then arranged for a valve to shut at the precise moment when the wave fell back, you would obtain a continuous uni-directional stream from what was originally an oscillating movement. With that stream you could in turn generate energy.

The 'valve' that Moray used was made of that rare mineral germanium that was to play such an important role in the transistor industry at a later stage. Moray was thus the first person to make practical use of this material. He said about it all, 'The universe is like an enormous broadcasting station.'

What was the energy found by Reich, Tesla and Moray? An association was founded in 1980 by Nieper, and it tries to collect all the data on this particular form of energy. They also gave it a new name, and called it 'tachyon energy'. They suspect that all heavenly bodies float in a gigantic 'tachyon' field and that one of the manifestations of the field is gravity. Making practical use of this energy would thus mean that you could obtain energy direct from gravity, an idea which has been used for a long time by science fiction writers. But just imagine that a practical application of such a transfer of energy is just around the corner. That every home, every town could simply gain access to such energy through means of transfer machines. The energy would have two characteristics — it would be completely free and it would cause no pollution. Only the apparatus would have to be supplied, but since there are no moving parts such a transformer could last say five hundred years. What an enormous social revolution all this would bring about!

For power is based on scarcity, but if for the first time in history scarcity were to be a thing of the past, then every worldly power would be humbled.

We can thus speak of energy waves which beat ceaselessly against the beaches of matter, whether these be galaxies, suns or planets. Energy waves which build up matter and hold the world together.

And now we return to the seraphim and their kadoosh . . . kadoosh . . . kadoosh . . .

Is it going too far to suppose that these waves of energy which eventually beat against our world as 'tachyon energy' find their origin there in the highest world? If that is so then the seraphim are doing something extremely wonderful. Then the holy . . . holy . . . holy is anything but monotonous work. In the first place not really a song of praise to the greatness of God. It is something else, literally the Song of Creation. The seraphim are the first who gather the waves of Creation emanating from God as through a lens and send it into space. And from their kadoosh . . . kadoosh . . . kadoosh the worlds are formed.

Immediately after the kadoosh comes 'the lord of Hosts'. The first word after kadoosh is the word one may not speak aloud if one is part of the Jewish world, and which is known as 'Jahweh' in Christianity. What is thrown up by the waves of creation? What is the essence? The great secret Name of God! The Name which the Jews say forms the foundation stone of the Creation.

Moray was a deeply religious man and one can imagine how deep was his reverence for the mighty beat of the waves of creation which came foaming up as surf against the material worlds. It is there, in the shadow of God, that the basic matter making up the worlds is sent away into space. This basic matter is then condensed a number of times. In the second heaven, the creative one, it is transformed into what are known as archetypes, the primeval examples for this world. In the first heaven, the formative one, they are transformed into matrices, the 'cake tins' of the material world. And finally they are condensed one last time to form the world we know. They are stored in tiny whirls which we call atoms. We perceive the energy as light, and also invisibly as waves of sound, radio waves, gravity waves and all other parts of the invisible spectrum.

From that surf of energy, derived from that highest world, is deposited the silt that we call the material worlds. It is fascinating to think about this onrushing energy. It is as if we hear those great waves, a continuous surf that gives us the feeling of weight on the spot where we stand.

Yet that energy cannot be called gravity or vibrations in that exalted world in which the seraphim have their existence. There it is of a much finer consistency. What is it then? Think of what the seraphim really are, the way points to the solution.

The holy . . . holy . . . holy of the seraphim is the beat of the waves of love! And that is of utmost importance. If a person really loves selflessly, then he is connected with this region. He has then become an ally and colleague of the seraphim. And then miracles happen, literally. That is not all that strange. The beat of the waves of love is the basic substance of this world. When you make a change, however small, right there at the source, then you see here, at the receiving end, enormous changes. Just as a small stone lying high up on a mountain can cause an enormous avalanche to fall down in the valley.

If someone really hands on a tiny bit of selfless love, that is the stone at the top of the mountain. It is as if a tiny trill of jubilation is added to the holy . . . holy . . . holy and then something on the earth down here is changed to the innermost fibre of its structure. The expression 'love conquers all' is then literally true.

Summing it all up we should be able to say that it is the name of God rather than the hydrogen atom which is the building material of the Universe. And that it is not the quantum, but holiness which forms the unit of energy. And love, not vibration is the substance of energy.

God's name, holiness and love are the foundations of the universe, and permeate the whole of Creation.

Cherubim

A second class of beings is also to be found near God.

Joost van den Vondel, the Dutch Shakespeare living in sixteenth-century Amsterdam, gave us this poem:

> Constantijntje, the happy little child,
> Little cherub from on high,
> Who looks down with a friendly smile
> On the idle acts of men.

In the original Dutch it is a charming little poem, but when Vondel speaks of his dead daughter as a 'little cherub from on high' he could hardly get his facts more wrong.

The word cherubim is a Hebrew word, the plural of Cherub, an awe-inspiring being.

The word is probably related to the word griffin, a mythological being made up from the upper parts of the body of an eagle and the lower parts of a lion, with pointed ears and a long tail. The animal is a heraldic beast. The prophet Ezekiel has left us a description of the cherubim. amongst other things he says in Ezekiel 1:

'They had the likeness of a man. And every one of them had four faces, and every one had four wings. And their feet were straight feet; and the sole of their feet was like the sole of a calf's foot: and they sparkled like the colour of burnished brass. And they had the hands of a man under their wings on their four sides.

'As for the likeness of their faces, they four had the face of a man, and the face of a lion on the right side: and they four had the face of an ox on the left side, they four also had the face of an eagle.

'As for the likeness of the living creatures, their appearance was like the burning coals of fire and like the appearance of lamps: it went up and down among the living creatures; and the fire was bright, and out of the fire went forth lightning.'

In Ezekiel (chapter 10) we see that this is about the cherubim. Quite remarkably, one of the people in my survey, a somewhat older woman, told me that she once had a vision of paradise. There were animals there who looked upwards at a glowing light she could not bear and there was a rainbow. (The rainbow was mentioned also by John the Evangelist.)

After this she was extremely happy and since then she has not been afraid to die, but she had never told this to anyone before. When I read her the relevant passage about the cherubim she was astonished, because she had never heard about it. John describes in the book of Revelation (chapter 4) about analogous beings. Only he gives them each six wings. And they call continually, day and night, 'Holy, holy, holy, Lord God Almighty, which was, and is, and is to come', just like the seraphim.

The differences between the descriptions given by Ezekiel and John are minor. It is obvious that they are talking about the same things.

The cherub is one of the first inhabitants of the heavens mentioned in the Bible and it was they who guarded the entrance to paradise from which Adam was driven out.

In Psalm 18, verse 11 (King James' version) we see God riding on a cherub, and 'celestial mount' could be one of the meanings of the word cherub.

We see the cherub yet again, this time in the form of sculpture. Two golden cherubim cover the Ark of the Covenant, the most holy object in the worship of Israel. When the high priest walked into the Holy of Holies, then God's voice was heard amongst the wings of the cherubim. Once again we have here the meaning 'God's mount'.

I have given as full a description as possible of these beings in order to show you how strange and other-worldly all this is. A guardian angel is nearly common-place compared to these awe-inspiring composite living beings.

Yet I do not believe that messages are given with the intention of not being understood by the people who receive them. Ezekiel, David and John saw those cherubim and thus it must be possible for our minds to penetrate this mystery, if only to a small degree.

The first thing we notice are the four faces. Even as an ornament we like to use this theme. I myself have an old-fashioned copper hand-bell with the four apostles on it. Above their four names one can see a lion, an ox, an angel and an eagle. These are the four fixed quarters of the Zodiac: Taurus, Leo, Scorpio and Aquarius. Very interesting, but we cannot get much further with this information.

You will notice that the lion, ox, angel and eagle on the copper bell do not quite agree with what Ezekiel describes as lion, ox, man and eagle. Behind this is the ancient knowledge that externally man and angel seem the same. You also see that in the above series of the signs of the Zodiac the third sign is not an eagle but a scorpion. That is because Scorpio is a double sign. On the one hand it has to do with death, that we see as symbolic of the scorpion; on the other hand it has to do with victory over death, and then we are dealing with the high-flying eagle. An interesting point in this context is that people who have many signs in Scorpio in their horoscope often have a pronounced eagle-eyed look.

Let us first spend a few moments thinking about the information we are given about the cherubim; God is mounted on a being with the four faces of the Zodiac's Taurus, Leo, Scorpio and Aquarius.

Since God has created everything, it thus becomes possible to say that everything probably has four sides to it and that — if you want to understand it at all — you must look at least at four sides of the problem. That is quite something.

We usually examine only one side — our own — and we are already quite proud when we remark wisely (usually to

11 'I beheld Satan as lightning fell from heaven'
(Luke 10:18)

to someone else) 'You should also see the other person's point of view'. This principle, that we hear the other side, forms the basis of law under a constitution.

Now it is not my intention to explain the astrological meanings of the four faces. What is important is that we understand that we must look in four directions if we are to understand anything of this world.

Let us take a man. You can look at his body in the way a surgeon or a laboratory does, as purely physical. That is known as the Taurus side.

You can look at him from a psychological point of view, with his ups and downs and his hidden corners. That is what is called the Scorpio side.

You can look at him spiritually: asking what is his way of looking at life, at what level is he? That is the Leo side.

And you can see the man from the heavenly point of view: is this man in contact with God? Does he pray? That is the Aquarius side.

With serious illnesses you must often examine all four levels and this is also important in problems about relationships. If one of the two partners is underdeveloped at one level, then the corresponding level of the other partner is left out in the cold.

In these times you see many women with a well-developed 'need for heaven' married to a husband almost completely lacking this quality. Then those women feel that their marriage is like a cardigan buttoned up the wrong way; not only is there always one button too many, but the whole cardigan hangs awry.

The political world is also ruled by the four levels. Take cruise missiles, for instance, which — seen from the purely military Scorpio level — are logical, though an unimaginable diasaster if seen from the highest level, that of a man as he is intended to be here. And by this I mean all cruise missiles, both of the East and of the West. And finally: the life of Jesus could be described only by four evangelists. Only then do you have the full measure of completeness. That is why the four Gospels do not quite agree with one another. No more than would the descriptions of four people around the four sides of a giant tree standing in the forest.

If the four Gospel stories were to agree exactly with each other, none of them would be true!

Ezekiel depicts the cherubim as beings that are covered in eyes. The Revelation of St John adds to this that they were full of eyes both on the outside and within. What could this mean?

Notice first the way it is mentioned, eyes both outside and within? Try that for yourself, my dear reader. Look at the words in front of you right now and at the same time cast your eyes within and regard yourself as you sit reading this. What do you notice? That your awareness has changed; it increases. You are really awake within yourself for just a moment. But that is all, as far as you are concerned, for you see only these words, and you see yourself reading these words.

But imagine that your awareness were to increase. You become aware of the book resting on your lap and of your skin which registers that pressure. You become aware of your breathing, of the self that registers that breathing. Of the colour of the carpet and of your reaction to that colour. In a way, you become full of eyes, both inside and on the outside.

You are now approximating what was written of the cherubim. They who are clearly aware of all details of Creation and simultaneously of the source from which the Creation comes. It means that in our Creation, however far removed some planets are from the centre, no parts exist which are not held fast in God's awareness. If the seething roar of the beating waves of Kadoosh, Kadoosh, Kadoosh were to cease but for a moment, then the world would vanish in the blink of an eye. That is the background to the curious remark that the hairs on our heads have been numbered (Matthew 10, verse 30).

They are not blind, but in fact totally aware forces which form the Creation. If one looks for the basic matter of our Creation, beyond the quanta and beyond the vibrations of energy, then one comes up not only against love but also against the fact that this is connected to a crystal clear intense awareness. An awareness which penetrates all details of Creation. This is an awesome thought.

The cherubim also call out Holy, Holy, Holy, but with them the emphasis is slightly different. If with the seraphim the emphasis is on love, with the cherubim it is on wisdom. This can be deduced from the position they take in the great ten-fold symbol of the heavenly regions we talked about before. The seraphim flood creation with the warmth of God, the cherubim with their clear intense awareness. This last is called the Logos, which has been with difficulty translated into our own language as 'the Word'.

Let us ponder over this creative word. The word that is formulated in God's awareness and that is sung by the cherubim.

Do not take that word to mean a cool matter-of-fact expression. We will take a very simple example and imagine that God wants to create a crocodile and that He formulates the word crocodile.

Then we must not just think of the anatomy of a crocodile with its impressive armour, its awesome power but we must also think that the good God enjoyed Himself in creating this horrifying beast. He pronounced the word 'crocodile' with great love, in the way we pronounce the name of a much-loved flower. Wisdom is always full of warmth. However, wisdom is difficult to perceive with our five senses. That perception teaches us that a crocodile is a monster that we shoot before it gets too big. We can then make handbags or shoes from its hide. Wisdom is learned in other ways. If you apply love to what surrounds you regardless of the reaction of those surroundings, wisdom is created.

You come across that wisdom sometimes in older people, who in the course of a long lifetime have not lost their love for others. It is sometimes formulated in a simple manner but it always contains the mildness of love. When I was doing my military service we had a colonel in charge of us who was one of the most stupid people I have ever come across. He had slowly risen to his own level of incompetence, and there he stayed. I could not bear the man.

Now we also had with us an older sergeant-major, the type that has a crew cut, a jack-of-all-trades. And every time I threatened to explode he would look at me with wise old eyes and say, 'Calm down, doc. If you want to ride rather than walk you have to endure the noise of an ass's braying.' With that remark he stopped me from doing a lot of silly things and created an atmosphere of tolerance that made it possible to endure working under the colonel. He gave me room to breathe.

You also come across such wisdom in those who have earnestly studied the word of God for a whole lifetime and (and what I am about to add is very relevant here) have also tried to apply it to their own lives. You recognise that principle in people's eyes. It is as if they distance themselves from the world and yet immediately bridge the gap with their great friendliness. The world can touch them but no longer break them. And they have become tolerant rather than cynical.

Ripe old fruit in the garden of earth.

Everyone who is associated with wisdom is also associated with cherubim. His word becomes charged even if he does not understand why this should be so. He obtains power. It reproduces itself. No wonder; resonance has occurred in the 'broadcast' sent out by the cherubim.

It all reminds me of the story that Aunt Corrie ten Boom liked to tell, about a woodpecker tapping at a tree trunk; and that very instant lightning struck the tree and the tree was sundered at the precise point tapped by the woodpecker. The bird flew off shaking its head and said to itself, 'I would never have thought that I had that much power in my beak.'

So it goes with people who take the words of the Bible seriously. Their words are in tune with the Word and are strengthened beyond measure. Then it can be that without being aware of it you can say a few words to someone in need and that many years later the person can say, 'Those words changed my life.' Only we must take care not to be like that woodpecker and think that the power is our own.

We must also take great care that we do not regard cherubim and seraphim as abstract forces. They are individual beings, living personalities, even more so that we are ourselves, who are still rather shadowy. Through love and wisdom it is possible to form bonds with these mighty living allies. And if you watch carefully you can notice their influence.

Thus I hope that nobody will ever think of a cherub as being that chubby angel in the cornice by the ceiling. Although I hasten to add for the sake of completeness that Swedenborg says that angels from the highest regions sometimes appear before us as children because they are so close to God and are thus so innocent.

Nonetheless it seems probable to me that should you even meet with a cherub he will certainly not look as complicated as in these descriptions. The cherub will probably also have a shining human form.

The four faces — of which three are those of animals — and the six wings must be seen as indications of properties, and not as literal external characteristics.

The Ophanim (literally, wheels)

Ezekiel tells us in his first chapter that near each of the cherubim there were many-coloured wheel-like structures. These wheels are built up in such a way that you saw, as it were, a wheel within a wheel. These wheels were lifted from the earth together with the cherubim and went with them everywhere. It was said that the 'spirit of the cherubim' was in these rings, which is as much as to say that they took their energy from the cherubim. Both ancient Hebrew and ancient Christian thought took these wheeled forms to be a separate angel hierarchy.

Since we are told that the inner wheel was 'full of eyes' we can see that they were not mechanical structures but that there was awareness within the wheels.

Take a little time to absorb that image. Multi-coloured, transparent rings, one turning within the other. The inner one with eyes, and they rise. Does that remind you of something?

I am of the opinion that we cannot avoid the issue. It is an almost exact description of a most mysterious phenomenon which people have noticed over a long period of time but which has increased explosively in the second half of the twentieth century. I am referring to what are known as UFOs. What they have in common has been noticed by others, and I mention this fact because it is one of the reasons why some people have drawn the conclusion that God was really as astronaut, a representative of a higher stellar race, who wanted to lift the ape-like inhabitant of this planet from his lowly state by tinkering with his heredity. And Who still comes from time to time to take a look at how His breeding colony is getting on.

That is a strange form of reasoning. For what you are doing is virtually pushing everything onto a materialistic plane. Then even the god or gods are material beings, even though they live a great distance away. In such reasoning there is no room for higher worlds.

If I went on reasoning logically, I would have to ask myself why angels coming from heaven do not carry oxygen masks. For after all, heaven begins just above Mount Everest, and every angel coming down would have to carry a space suit at the very least.

A second difficulty is this: If we think the gods were no more than astronauts, who made these astronauts?

No, if we really want to understand the world then we will have to make use of higher worlds, the heavens. Then we must allow our understanding to rise right up to seraphim, cherubim and ophanim. The question now is, 'What are UFOs?' Do they really have anything to do with the ophanim? Ten per cent of all people living today have seen a UFO. What do they see? It is well known that UFOs can vanish suddenly. That is called dematerialisation. And science fiction writers hasten to add that they materialise once more in a distant galaxy, so that one tremendous jump can bridge light years.

It is a fascinating theory, but is it true? Or do we see in the air simply symbolic representations of the ophanim, just as Ezekiel saw?

And do we, with our technologically-based way of thinking, make of this just a machine?

Or do UFOs have nothing to do either with the ophanim or with the travellers from other planets? Are they perhaps expressions of that same mysterious 'in-between' race of which previous centuries knew much more and which they referred to as elves? Many UFO stories sound as if they are mischief, tom-foolery, and those are constant elements of stories about elves.

I do not therefore give a solution to the riddle of UFOs, but I would like to point out that they have a strange similarity to the ophanim of Ezekiel, which are referred to by Dionysius as the third race of angels. And something like that does not happen without a reason.

Even if it appeared that UFOs are not manifestations of ophanim, then we should still allow for the fact that we are being powerfully reminded of the structure of the ophanim, because UFOs do look like them. Let us suppose then that they are at least related.

The ophanim have another name in the Dionysian system, Thrones.

It is a strange idea, that an angel hierarchy should look like a wheel. But do not forget that these are living symbols. After all, John referred to Christ as a lamb, yet he looked human. Do not get too attached to the symbol and do not think, 'What a dreadful idea that a living being should look like that'.

If you met an ophanim face to face, you would simply meet a being with a human appearance. The wheel structure is more or less a family coat-of-arms. A flag that covers the contents. Where are these Thrones or ophanim to be found on our ten-fold charts of the heavens? In which heavenly region do they live? Exactly as Ezekiel already mentioned, they stand next to the cherubim. They inhabit a region about which something strange is told. It is said that in that part of heaven, manifested matter was first laid out.

When we speak of cherubim and seraphim with their three-fold 'holy', one cannot really speak of matter. One speaks rather of the mighty irresistible waves of the concept of creation. It is only in the region of the ophanim that matter first starts to condense. Exactly like the first layer of ice in a ditch.

Let us build this up carefully. Imagine that you have an idea in your head. The idea of creating a foal from modelling clay. You can visualise the foal in your mind's eye, but it is still purely an idea. It takes up no space anywhere. But

164

now you start really modelling it in clay. Now it has 'materialised'. Now it does take up space. Anywhere that something materialises, space is taken up. That clay foal will not last for ever. One day it will crumble and return to dust. If something is made to exist materially, then in the long run it will vanish again. There is a 'before' and an 'after'. As soon as space appears, time also appears. Those twin concepts of time and space first appear around the ophanim. They do not have any meaning around the cherubim, but they become a reality when near the ophanim.

Now you will all have observed that there is something strange and special about time.

Our first impression is that time passes in a straight line. But if we look carefully we see that each Sunday is eventually followed by another Sunday, that every spring is eventually follower by another spring, that particular phases return to our lives over and over again. Time actually turns round in a circle, or perhaps in a spiral, since you never return to exactly the same point.

Subjectively, the circle also lies clearly in front of us. Everyone who has lost someone through death will know of the extra pain you feel in the weeks which commemorate the death of the loved person. If your mother died in August you are further away from her death in February than in August a year later.

It is thus possibly very relevant that the angel hierarchy which deals with time and space could be indicated by a circular structure.

An incredibly important area is covered by the work of the Thrones.

Possibly they help to condense that which comes to them as an idea in to real matter, just as we condensed our idea of a foal to form a clay foal (although of course, in our case the clay was already present). And as soon as matter is present you can start to speak of the force of attraction of that matter, of the force of gravity. And look where all this will lead us.

The most recent theories in physics teach us that there is an intrinsic connection between three concepts; these are in fact our visible world of matter, gravity and time.

Naturally you have heard that matter is made of the most incredibly small units called atoms. In the same way we see nowadays that light is also composed of very small units called quanta. And this has been taken even farther. It is said the waves of gravity are made up of very small particles and these are given the complicated name of 'tachyons'. And people now think that these tachyons are the real building blocks of the material creation. That they are the real foundation of atoms.

What a strange world is described in this way by modern physics when it is talking about very small particles. Thus it is stated that tachyons move very fast and that, if they start moving faster, time is compressed and if they move more slowly time is stretched.

This is not something we can visualise, even if we know perfectly well that time can sometimes seem to be passing quickly or slowly, according to whether we are interested or bored.

The new physics thus sees time not as something illusive or abstract, but as something extremely concrete and thus we have really come back to the ancient Hebraic ideas which considered time as something as substantial as water.

What I really want to say with all this is that modern physics makes a direct connection between gravity, time and that which we see in this world of appearances. And that the Thrones or ophanim occupy the position in Creation where these three things first materialise, i.e. the ordering of space, gravity and time.

I warn you that these things are beyond our understanding. The despair of physics is that it cannot understand its own discoveries. They go beyond the understanding of human brains. That is why any conception you may try to make is totally wrong. I can just imagine that the tremendous stream of Creation condenses around the Thrones after it has passed through the seraphim and cherubim. I can suppose the Thrones cause the stream of Creation to revolve and that these whirls are condensed in the second heaven lying beneath, and again in the first heaven below the second and eventually land up as an extremely fast swirling in our own world. And these are the atoms, which we know are actually made up from energy whirling round and round at top speed, even if matter does seem to us to be so rigid and unmoving.

I understand that I have pushed the reader to the limit with all these considerations. However, here we find ourselves at a dizzying height.

We should really be released momentarily from the power of gravity that holds down our bodies and our thoughts. People talk a lot these days about antigravity and speculate that UFOs fly by that power. We need a great deal of antigravity to allow our thoughts to elevate up to the third heaven.

Do the ophanim help us by their deeds? Or are they so closely tied to the Creation that they are too exalted for us? Well now, I believe that they are intimately tied to us. Our material body is made up of small whirling atoms, so we are tied to the ophanim from the depths of our material being. But it is also quite possible that a man like Moray, whose ideal was to use gravitational fields for clean and cheap energy, drew his inspiration from the ophanim. Perhaps every person who tries to put the matter of this earth to as good a purpose as is possible has made a connection with these austere angels. The fight against polluting fossil energy and the even more dangerous atomic energy will be won only by those who make some union with the angel hierarchy that stands at the cradle of matter.

I must try your patience a little longer. It is necessary for you to learn yet another Hebrew word. It is the word 'galgal', used by Ezekiel as an alternative to ophanim, also meaning wheel.

The word galgal has, in Hebrew, a double meaning, namely that of both wheel and of pupil of the eye. Thanks to the pupil of our eye, the image of the outer world is formed on our retina. But that is reasoned by us, the receivers of that image. Just imagine that the galgal, the pupils there in the highest heaven, are an image of God's eyes, which He turns on His Creation. This is not done just in order to allow the image of the Creation to impinge on Him so that He can say to Himself that 'it was good'. It was also done in order to project the world through those pupils to the outside, just as we project a film through a lens.

Then the Thrones would really be God's eyes. And the strange thing is that people have always had in mind the great eye of God looking at the Creation. Some churches have this enormous eye painted high up above the congregation where it looks down on everyone.

Let us take another look at all we have discovered about the three highest hierarchies. We see a division of labour:

The seraphim send out a carrier wave that vibrates, forming the bass tone of this world.

The cherubim modulate this carrier wave and transform it into a symphony.

The ophanim condense the symphony into a visible creation. Not independently, but in continuous, intimate contact with the Creator Himself, so that one could say, 'God thinks and it is, God speaks and it appears.'

My tale about the ophanim would not be complete if I did not mention that the world galgal (pupil) is related to the world 'gilgul', which means, the return of particular things. Ancient Hebrew thinking formulated something similar to reincarnation. Thus it was said that Abraham was a reincarnation or gilgul, of Adam. But it was not all quite as easy as the concept of reincarnation that we encounter in current popular literature, where for instance, I am the reincarnation of a Tibetan priest who is in turn the reincarnation of an Atlantean priest.

Hebrew ideas on the subject held that different parts of a person could return in different positions; someone's head to one person, someone's soul to another, so that what forms a unity in me is then divided over a number of people. A disturbing thought but then it should not be taken literally, in fact probably something entirely different is meant. These matters are discussed in order to focus the listener's attention on the fact that the whole of humanity, whether spread out over space in any given era, or spread out through the whole history of existence of this earth, forms a unity. Thus it is that some freely translate the word 'adam' as 'humanity'. We are all related much more intimately with each other and our forebears than we would at first think.

And ponder on the fact that three of the four faces of the cherub are the faces of animals. Is this not an indication that we are not only closely bound to one another but also to the whole animal kingdom? Are we not most emphatically coming to see the fact that the whole Creation is a unity, something which the new science of ecology is only slowly discovering in the course of the last ten years?

Yes, and just look at our civilisation. A civilisation that in order to obtain its energy can only brutally tear apart the atoms that form the building blocks of matter. Would we wound the ophanim with this? Is that why the image of wheels appears so often in the clouds, as a warning not to continue in this way?

We have had to develop all these ideas in connection with the three highest angel hierarchies, and that is only a fraction of what could be further considered about them.

It is really quite something, that world up there in the

shadow of God. Just imagine for a moment that if the seraphim and cherubim did not sound the 'Holy, Holy, Holy, Lord God Almighty' for the space of one single minute, and if the ophanim were to shut their eyes momentarily, then your family, your house, your garden, your planet, your starry sky, your sun and moon, and last but not least, you yourself would vanish as if you had never been.

The world of God's shadow is thus in a way much less distant that you might think. You yourself live in God's shadow. The art is purely that of realising this constantly.

We can now set out the whole structure of the hierarchies once more.

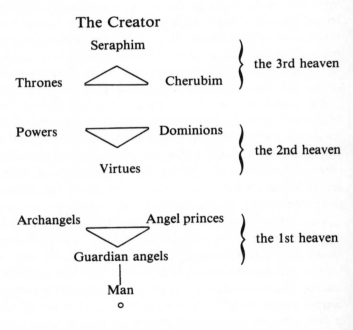

The Creator

Seraphim

Thrones   Cherubim   } the 3rd heaven

Powers   Dominions   } the 2nd heaven

Virtues

Archangels   Angel princes   } the 1st heaven

Guardian angels

Man
o

There is much that can be said about this structure but that goes beyond the scope of this book. I would, however, like to make two remarks; in the order of conscious beings it is apparent to us that man stands on the bottom rung. Thus, he is not the peak of consciousness as some evolutionists think; he is so only on earth. That takes him down a peg or two from his throne, but he is obviously something else. He is the tenth angel hierarchy. Man is an angel in the making and the sooner he realises this the better it will be for us all.

Perhaps people say, 'But that is not what I want.' That, then, is a pity, because this is the proof that he belongs to those beings that are aware. He can say 'No'. If an angel says 'No' to a task then he becomes a fallen angel. We do not therefore have to do much searching in order to find out in which category we belong as persons: to the exalted or to the fallen angels. But someone who has fallen can get up again. It would appear to be serious but not hopeless.

The second remark is about God. It is considered a sign of spiritual progress these days if, in intellectual circles, you identify God as a 'sublime thought' or as 'pure Being'. I think this conception misses the point. To think about God as being a sublime, abstract thought is sacrilege. It is not 'far out' or 'spiritual', it is distorted and very mundane. In the way a mathematical expression is mundane. It is true that it is written that no one has ever seen God, but that is not the same as saynng that He has no form. Nobody has ever really seen another human being. The form covers the 'other', and that 'other' looks out of his eyes for an instant, but only on special occasions. Or you hear that 'other' every now and then in his voice or from a gesture. The inner being is hidden inside a man and is also hidden in God.

If God appears to man then he chooses to cover His unimaginable greatness with the simple outward form of a human being. If God appears to us then it is as the suffering servant of a human race rushing to its corruption. In the Old Testament He appeared to Adam as He walked round the Garden. And to Abraham as the mysterious priest-king Melchidezek. The Jews expect Him as the King Messiah. He appears in the New Testament as Jesus Christ. He whom the Christians expect a second time is the same One whom the Jews expect the first time. He appears as a simple, friendly man who is full of love. A man in the likeness of Adam, of humanity. A man who, when Adam had eaten from the forbidden tree, did not angrily shout, 'What have you done now?' but instead asked gently, 'Adam where are you?' (as if He did not know). And when Jonah was furious with God for not having destroyed Nineveh and had just made him, Jonah, look foolish with his prediction of doom, he said softly, 'Are you really justified in getting so angry?' Instead of 'Jonah, stop moaning.' Or think of Job who had the gall to say to God, 'I call on you to appear in court as a witness against yourself that you have treated me unfairly.'

And then God showed Job the wonders of His Creation. 'Not very sporting of God', decided Jung. 'Job did not get an answer.' But this was not so. Job got his first lesson in ecology and saw that there were much larger frameworks than he had ever realised into which his little miseries fitted in a miraculous fashion.

Think of Abraham who started some sort of horse-trading with God so as to save Sodom and Gomorrah from destruction. 'If I should find fifty just men, would you allow the cities to perish? Surely not?' And God allows the trading to go on. Abraham beats him down and down to a final figure of ten just men. Did all this give pleasure to God, as Abraham stood there pleading, in the way a man takes pleasure in his son?

Take God in human form. Is that not profane? No, on the contrary. God understood as a formless abstraction, that is profane. When we have done with all the angel rulers, the pomp and circumstance, the splendour, all that is left is the man full of love with arms spread wide. It is too simple to be true, a folly. Perhaps that is why Lucifer thought it might be a good idea to depose God. Perhaps that is why so many people feel themselves drawn to the non-Biblical religions. These at least spur people to climb ever upwards and promise them ever greater initiations into ever deeper secrets which are not accessible to ordinary people. With at the end of it all a God who is only an abstract light, a smile without a cat as in 'Alice in Wonderland'. For those who do not know the story: Alice saw a grinning cat sitting in a tree when suddenly the cat disappeared but the grin stayed behind.

Actually God is also, when appearing as a simple man, an insult to all those high climbers. Because just imagine that you have undergone the most terrible privations in the course of a hundred lives in order to climb an endlessly high tower stretching to heaven. In the first life you buy an entrance ticket from a simple porter and then you climb and climb. And finally you arrive, in the course of your hundredth life, at the top, and you open the gate of paradise, and to your joy you see a great angel who says solemnly, 'I shall personally conduct you to God's presence.' And then he takes you to a little pond and there, on a bench, by the side of the water, sits the simple porter who sold you the ticket which you bought in your first life. You think, 'How has he got here, this must be a mistake', and then the porter says to the angel, 'Thank you, Gabriel, that will be all. Leave him to me', and then he turns round to you and says in a friendly tone, 'What took you so long? I have been sitting waiting here for all of ninety-nine lifetimes!'

Would you not feel as if you had been cheated? Had you not expected something much higher, something better, something more worthy than that porter, after all the trouble you took. No, if you are such a climber you would not feel drawn to such a simple humane God.

I myself am no such climber for I am afraid of heights. That is why I am very pleased to find that the porter has come down and is offering another route to paradise. A route for people such as me, people with little holiness and a great fear of heights. Actually, it is impossible for me to love an abstract God. Just as it is impossible for me to love Pythagoras' theorum. But a God who, with incomprehensible modesty, appears as a man, why yes, I can love him very much.

I believe we should be allowed to take the statement that we are made in the image of God much more literally than is usually admitted. If we are indeed created in His image then it not only says something about us but also about Him. It tells us what He looks like should we meet Him and it also explains why most celestial beings look so human.

The human shape is the shape of God.

Whichever way you go, the way of the climbers or the way of the people with a fear of heights, after passing by all the great ones of the earth and the heavens, after one life or many, eventually you reach the simplicity of God and He faces you with a choice. To take on His appearance and stay simple and subservient to all eternity or to take on the appearance of the prime father of all fallen angels and become a grandee in the kindgom of despair. Free will is the basis of the relationship between Creator and created. That is the very reason why He takes on a simple form when appearing to us. Should we see Him as He is inside for but the tiniest instant, we would be totally consumed. God becoming man is an unimaginable blessing for we weak people.

Because God has also the aspect of 'all-consuming fire', that is why Christ 'covered over' God. In Christ, God protects us from Himself.

We have now gone through all the heavens and have penetrated to the beginning. First we saw people looking to heaven, to the guardian angels and what lay beyond. And now, at the end of this voyage, we see a human form which radiates oceans of love. Beginning and ending locked into

174

one another. The furthest heaven is the nearest. The cherubim live in the highest heaven but if all is well, then God lives in your heart.

But because this book is about angels I must now put the question, 'How are we to regard angels, if God Himself appears to be the guide and companion of people?' There exists an expression that God created mothers because he could not appear everywhere at the same moment. This is of course great nonsense, for that is exactly what he can do, and still have all the time in the world left over. It is not intended that we put angels in the place of God; that we worship and honour them and regard them as being our aid in times of peril or need. That is not what they are. They are inhabitants of the spiritual world, and, just as we are, they are fellow servants of God. They can be sent to pass on messages or to help, and they have regulatory and guiding tasks. Thus we find mentioned in the Zohar that there is a special angel called Sangariah in charge of those people on earth who are engaged in fasting (Book IV, 207a).

I believe it is true to say that the further we go along the path of God, the more angels we shall encounter on the path. The guiding hand behind them all is that of a God who is so modest that we are inclined to overlook His existence. A man who, when He walked on this earth, testified of Himself, 'I am meek and lowly of heart' (Matthew 11, verse 29).

Is that possible? Could God be so simple, friendly and full of love? Ought we not to be overcome and appalled by that other aspect of Him which created galaxies and atoms? Then you can admire Him enormously for these words without loving Him in any way. You can love Him for what He Himself is. For His simplicity, for His willingness to put Himself out for the least of His creations. Then God, as the good Shepherd who searches all around looking for the one lost sheep, is nearer to us than God the builder who appoints the stars to their places.

Do you remember the film, 'The Green Pastures'? It is about the dream, during Sunday School, of a little black boy. His gaze wanders outside, to the white clouds. On the clouds sit large black men with white wings who are fishing. Everywhere there are black angels, and everything is simple beautiful. And then suddenly everybody gets up.

An arch is formed by some of the clouds, and God Himself arrives. He wears a worn suit that is a little too tight and a somewhat shabby top hat on His grey curly hair. It is the old minister of the Sunday School, for that is how the little boy imagines God looks.

I believe, fifty years after I saw the film, that the little black boy had understood more of God than many a famous guru who teaches us to think about God in such an abstract way that we can only admire ourselves for being able to understand it.

God, just as simple and full of love as that old Sunday School teacher. It is enough to make you laugh. Well, that is all right, as long as it is a laugh of relief. It is all too much. You do not have to meditate any more, you need not travel to India or wear orange clothes, you only have to love a God who travels and suffers with you as an ordinary man and who loves all the people round you because He calls all these people His children.

I am sorry, a Dutchman can never pass up an opportunity for giving a sermon. We are now at the top of the church tower. Mind the ballustrade, it is not all that safe. Above us is the incomprehensible Creator, below us the hierarchies, and next to us the guide. It all seems soundly put together. Why has it then so obviously gone wrong?

That is the subject of the next chapter.

5. The Battle in Heaven

Old tales tell us of a tremendous battle that was supposed to have taken place in heaven. One section of angels, led by Lucifer, appeared to have rebelled against the Lord of Hosts, and was therefore thrown out of heaven by the angels who stayed true to God, under their leader Michael. The subject never fails to keep the human mind occupied. Breughel the Elder has painted the battle in great detail and he is but one of many.

Dante placed the fallen Lucifer in the deepest hell, not in one of the fiery furnaces but in an icy, freezing cold.

Lorber, the visionary, says something totally different. He supposes that Lucifer was the first living creation of God and that the intention had been that the universe would be populated from him in a harmonious way. But when he fell, he and his followers were transformed into matter. And in reality all matter which we — wherever we find ourselves in the material world — can perceive, is nothing other than the fallen angels which have been transmuted into congealed matter. The tragedy of it all — I am still referring to Lorber's ideas — is that all the spirits implied in Lucifer's being with the intention of setting them free at a later stage as independent spirits, were imprisoned in matter at the same time. And that the plan for salvation consists of winning back the myriad spirits and freeing them from congealed matter. There comes but one single moment in their existence when they walk around as a free human being and must make a conscious decision for the old fallen angel or for the Lord who wants to rescue them.

It is a remarkable opinion but I set it out here in order to show you that people are always intensively busy thinking about the powers of the fallen angels.

Rudolf Steiner has a different opinion about matter. He says that the congealed matter is of the ophanim and that these ophanim have lovingly offered this basis for our material existence.

The two opinions of Lorber and Steiner do not differ as much as people might think. Steiner concentrates his vision on the foundations of matter, as could have begun with the ophanim. Whereas Lorber tells us about the way matter has become much harder than was originally intended because of the Fall that occurred. Since people have discovered, through the findings of modern astronomical research, that there is an 'empty' path between the planets Mars and Jupiter and that in this path enormous fragments of material circle round the sun, they have deduced that a planet burst into fragments, and immediately further speculations have been put forward that this was the place where the famous battle of heaven took place.

Naturally, it is difficult to come to a decision about this since we were not there at the time. But we can do something else. We can start with our current situation, and then one thing becomes very clear: apart from the powers that take our part, there are powers that work against us. Let us first examine this in our personal life.

Every person who reads this, without exception, will agree with me that he or she does things in his or her life with the best of intentions. You must be really twisted if you deliberately try to do evil. Anyone who does is in need of psychiatric treatment.

And yet, you must also agree with me that few of those good intentions seem to succeed. It is even true that those people who love each other most can hurt each other the greatest. It is for this reason that Christianity stresses the fact that man is a fallen creature and that there is, even seen from a non-religious point of view, little to be said in his favour. But it will also be clear to everyone that evil, whether at a national or at a personal level, has a tendency to escalate. The person who releases evil soon loses control over it, and it quickly starts an independent career. It is interesting to note that many murderers declare to the judge that they had not intended to kill the other person and it is also noticeable that a quarrel tends to draw in those not personally involved, that a war can be started on a small scale and despite all efforts of the United Nations it escalates and that ever more terrible weapons are employed.

Evil leads its independent life if you give it the chance and thus the most obvious conclusion is that it has a life of its own and only tries to manifest itself through man.

It is also clear that the advance of humanity is seriously thwarted at every point of its possible development. This obviously becomes most clear at those points where people act who want to help to further the spiritual development of man. Persecution ensues immediately and automatically. Nearly all Old Testament prophets came to a violent end and Jesus Christ, who was, from a Christian point of view, a manifestation of God Himself, was crucified. And look at all those people in the history of Europe who tried to purify religion of materialistic influences or idolatry. They too were doggedly persecuted and put to death with great cruelty.

We see this remarkable retarding and persecuting force at work in other areas too. New breakthroughs in medicine were derisively waved aside, new political insights were swept under the carpet, new discoveries about energy were hushed up. To all appearances there are forces at work that do not bear goodwill to mankind.

In our analogy of treasure seakers on the bottom of the sea we could say that there are not only the helpful spirits who provide us with oxygen, information and other necessities, but that at the bottom of the sea live intelligent monsters of evil intent who regard every treasure on the sea bed as their property and every intruder as a tasty bite.

And now is the time to tell you what happened next with the wonderful clean energy first used by Tesla and discovered anew by Reich and Moray.

Tesla was a crafty old fox and kept his discovery a secret. But Reich, realising what a primal force he had discovered — he even caused an earthquake once — published his findings.

The FDA (Food & Drug Administration), one of the largest bureaucratic bodies in America, challenged him to appear in court. It was a strange case. Reich had generated energy — quite a lot of it in fact — without using fossil fuel, without running a windmill, or without other obvious energy-generating equipment. That energy then appeared to come from nothing. The judge decided that Reich had done something that he was not able to do, that therefore Reich was a confidence trickster and he ordered him to stop his researches.

When Reich carried on despite this ruling (his actual profession was as a psychiatrist) he was put in jail. He died there at the beginning of 1957. In that same year the Food & Drug Administration managed to obtain a court order that Reich's books and discoveries were to be officially burned. Even in 1960 books of Reich were burned in the municipal incinerator of the city of New York (Energy & Character, Jan. 1972).

This, my dear reader, as you can see did not take place in the Middle Ages somewhere in a dark castle, but in 1960 in the United States of America. Now do you understand what I mean by the forces that hold back development? If everything had not been properly documented this would have been thought too unbelievable to have attention paid to it.

But what about Moray? He allowed all those 100-watt light bulbs to burn in front of witnesses by tuning his apparatus to cosmic energy. How did he get on and where is his apparatus?

Why do we still go on muddling through the oil crisis? Did Moray have no friends to help him distribute his apparatus on a large scale? No, Moray did not have many friends. There was one, called Lovesy, who said that whatever happened, he would help Moray. Unfortunately you have to watch out if you say things like that in this world, since he had not reckoned on being helped out of this world in a mysterious manner.

Later, the American government sent a man called Frazer who examined the apparatus from all sides for months on end and then one day used a large axe to chop it all into small fragments.

Moray escaped attempts to murder him on three occasions, simply because he could shoot better than his assassins. Moray died after the war, deeply disappointed that he had not been able to leave humanity with a clean and cheap form of energy.

Before we go further into these opposing forces, I would like you to reflect for a moment on what would have happened if this gravity-energy had become common knowledge on our planet. You would have gigantic decentralisation, many taxes would have become superfluous, capitalism would have been abolished because everyone would have become a capitalist, and communism and socialism for the same reason. It would be as if every person had a fierce mountain stream next to his home which he used to generate electricity. And the strange thing is that the stream really is right there. In other words, the power of gravity. And basically we know that this form of energy can be used, and that its practical application is only a matter of time.

Robert Jungk showed quite clearly in his book 'The Atom State' that the change to nuclear energy will logically lead to the formation of a hard and authoritarian police state.

But what would a massive development of this other type of energy lead to? To a great freedom of the people and to a planetary situation where the worst war would be over the American Cup? Or would man start murdering once more out of boredom? Or in order to defend some new ideology?

Is it true that only a new type of man could 'take on' such a new form of energy? The free availability of a clean form of energy which costs nothing is something that is far beyond our imagination as far as the consequences are concerned. But that is not the reason why I set down these stories here. It is up to humanity itself how it makes use of these gifts. But, that it would be a gift, is obvious without further explanation. The pollution of the air would cease, as would the curse of the high base rate of interest and the unbearable weight of bureaucracy, and indeed, so much more. In whose name would you oppress man if he lived contentedly with this readily available energy, just as in distant islands satisfied inhabitants live contentedly on fish and coconuts?

I thus regard Tesla, Reich and Moray as positively inspired people and it is clear that those who imprisoned Reich and burned his books and those who destroyed Moray's apparatus and shot him, were negatively inspired people.

An inspiration is not something a human being gets because he is put together in such a wonderful way, but because he literally inspires — breathes in — so that inspiration flows towards him. You could say that there are evil powers who would love, above all else, to destroy the whole of humanity, or perhaps preferably enslave it, in this life as well as after our death. They inspire people with terrible discoveries such as hydrogen bombs and nerve gasses, police states and concentration camps and wherever they think they stand a chance they oppose all good impulses. Impulses such as the discovery of energy sources that are friendly to the environment, ecological insights, tolerant political systems and all the other possibilities of getting humanity out of its mess.

Wicked inspirations thus do not come from abstract forces. The forces of evil are affected by fallen angels, they who are inspired to fury at humanity because they themselves are bound and they envy the freedom of the other. As a kind of dark mirror image of the heavenly hierarchies, the hierarchies of fallen angels stretch below us. Inspirations stream towards us from above and from below.

Who is that Lucifer really, the old enemy of the human race, with his host of fallen angels? Hebrew thought calls him and his cohorts the 'rind' because they fell from the kernel. They have become totally outside.

According to me it is rarely realised that the old enemy of mankind was once a cherub.

Again it is Ezekiel who, in his 28th chapter, leaves us a description of this being. At first sight it seems as if Ezekiel is writing about the King of Tyre, but old texts frequently hide such important information amongst such mundane description. There appears before our very eyes a 'guardian cherub' in the Garden of Eden. He is covered with splendid precious stones, is full of wisdom and beauty, is perfect in his ways.

And then, all of a sudden, an unimaginable disaster occurs — he falls, and this is ascribed to his pride.

For the sake of completeness I must add here that in the apocryphal book of Bartholomew the evil spirit is called the first of the created archangels, who is called Sataniel before his Fall, and Satan afterwards. (Easily understood if one knows that the suffix 'el' means God.)

Is the evil one a fallen cherub or a fallen archangel? We do not know and it is quite typical of the nature of the power

184

of evil that even his derivation is not clear. Evil often characterises itself by its vagueness.

When we read in old legends or tales or tidings that a gigantic battle once took place in heaven, then we must realise that these describe eternally ruling principles. The armies of Michael and Lucifer still oppose each other, for in the heavenly regions we are dealing with an eternal present. The battle between these two armies is not really a thing of the past — if we look carefully at our world's history — but is still going on. There are centuries during which the struggle quietens down and there are centuries when Michael and Lucifer are at it again with full fury. Ours is such a period, and then it becomes necessary to choose sides, to know from whom we derive our inspiration. Does one want the pure mountain air of Michael or the smell of corpses that is Lucifer. Neutrality, as Mr Cohen taught us, no longer exists.

However, it is not all that simple to recognise an inspiration. From which region does it come? Does this spirit belong to heaven or to hell? The evil spirits of inspiration have the utmost cunning and like to present themselves as benefactors of humanity. And who are those who listen? One thing has become clear to me. Those fighting against the enslavement of humanity are not the ones in the places of power. They are often small groups of well-intentioned people without power and with quiet strength. They go about in friendship with each other, maybe coming from very different backgrounds. They do not have to be — in the orthodox meaning of the word — religious. While all those who endeavour to enslave humanity have a totally different appearance.

Jungk sets down a few characteristics: in the company of enthusiastic defenders of real human values they are bored, cool, arrogant, irritated, without a trace of warmth or friendliness.

Wicked spirits make use of rational arguments, preferably covered in a layer of piety. That is how the first atom bomb was built in the United States, starting with the reasoned argument that Hitler was likely to formulate the same plan. After the war it was discovered that Hitler had indeed had the same idea but that the nuclear scientists under him had sabotaged the plan. Totally logical reasoning of the leaders of the United States led to the release of hell.

It is a huge mistake to think that wicked spirits are not religious. You believe that God is One? How right you are, the devils also believe and tremble, says St James in chapter 2, verse 19.

Atheism is only a transitional phase, and is not really useful to the spirits of evil. It is the phase of gradual loosening from heaven. The real purpose of wicked inspiration is the worship of evil.

Fortunately there is one sure way to recognise from which direction the wind is blowing. Hell always wants to dominate. As soon as you see the desire for domination coupled to what is supposed to be an enlightened idea, you should become suspicious. Instead of the abolition of the proletariat, there is the dictatorship of the proletariat, and instead of a co-operative, an establishment. Stated in even simpler terms: Hellish inspiration sooner or later leads to suspicion and hate, and eventually to oppression and murder. Heavenly inspiration leads to mutual trust and love.

We are not weak victims of the angelic choirs and hellish cacophonies stretching above and below us. We are free to choose, and that is one of the greatest wonders of the Creation.

However we cannot say, 'I am not going to get involved.' If we do, then evil will involve us, often in a violent manner.

We are quite definitely faced with a choice, and a conscious one at that. Our freedom consists of saying 'yes' or 'no' to goodness or to evil. It does not lie in refusing the choice as we are not born to drift like jelly fish.

But it remains very important that if we say 'yes', this choice is not made in such a way that we subject ourselves as a slave to a master. Strangely enough, if we say 'yes' to heaven, the angels go out of their way to allow us total freedom to make our own decisions. We remain the active operator and we are permitted to make our decisions in freedom.

If, on the contrary, we say 'yes' to evil inspiration, then hell will do its utmost to push us down and make us into an inspired slave.

That is why certain religions are clearly recognised as being the worship of an evil spirit. The members of such a sect have become slaves without a will of their own in the hands of a leader who can literally demand anything at all from his followers, from prostitution to suicide. Belief is never blind, but superstition is always so.

There is a noticeable parallel with the cancer question. It has been found that many cancer patients have a particular character structure. They have become voluntary slaves of their environment, and that environment is complacently pleased. Mother is the slave of everyone, even of her married children. A man is slave to his company, and because of his unremitting zeal for work, he is the only one who knows it all, he is irreplaceable. And then the husband of the mother gets carried away at the office party or the man's business takes a turn for the worse and the worlds of these people collapse. Everything they lived for has become relative, life is not worth living, their power of resistance breaks down and the cancer begins its growth.

You have to teach such people that they must never allow control of their lives to slip out of their own hands. They must not allow themselves to be used by whoever or whatever but they themselves must live. They must feel that there is freedom for them too, and a mother should leave the mess to its own devices just for once and for Heaven's sake take the afternoon off to spend as she likes and that a man should devote some more time to that hobby that used to fascinate him so much.

Is that not developing a form of self-centredness? No, it is a development that leads to greater internal freedom. And that is not contrary to God's will, as we do sometimes believe in our community if we are still believers. The emphasis is laid so much on loving one's neighbour that one is inclined to forget that what was written was 'Love your neighbour as you love yourself.' That also is part of it all.

We are here on earth to practise love, that is one of the purposes of the training planet called Earth. But we must also practise freedom since love and freedom should go together.

It is heaven which encourages this freedom and it is wicked inspiration which continually urges us towards slavery. Preferably voluntary slavery, then you do not have any trouble with rebels later on.

That is the struggle in heaven within us all. The struggle for that will of ours which becomes freer as we turn to face upwards and less free as we face downwards.

Let me repeat Moray's statement, 'The universe is like an enormous radio broadcasting station'.

That is splendid. If that is true then there is not only a humanity which receives but also a crew to man the broadcasting station. And I mean that as literally as possible.

Now I would like to warn you away from the idea that the battle in heaven is an engagement of two equally strong armies that fight eternally, with the human soul as the battlefield. You easily fall into what was once the Persian way of seeing the world in terms of spirits of light and darkness who are evenly matched and where neither ever gains the victory.

This dualistic vision of the world is very probably incorrect. It was actually overthrown even before this Persian conception came to its full bloom, namely in one of the oldest books in the Bible — the book of Job. There you are shown God Himself having a quiet talk with Satan, the obstructor. He even manages to get God to the point where He allows him, Satan that is, to arrange for the good Job to be overcome by a series of disasters.

It thus seems that this world, which appears to us as dualistic, is in fact united within God. Even Satan has his task in all this, though it may be a very tragic one. Perhaps that is the reason why Michael did not dare to utter an accusation, as we have discussed. You do not kick a fallen brother when he is down. Just because of the constant obstruction, definite victories are gained here on earth from time to time. Muscles are strengthened, powers are toughened, a man is given back-bone.

Even that arch-obstructor has a task to fulfill in this enormous universe, perhaps without his knowledge, although we must not underestimate his intelligence. He is constantly testing human material, just as steel is tested in a steel mill before it is sold.

We must resist Satan with force, that is our duty. But let us be like Michael and not be too quick to cast aspersions on him, let alone heap him with curses. Even he is a creation of God and we may assume that — even in the case of this fallen angel — God has not allowed things to get out of hand.

6.   The Scent of Jasmine

We now go back to our old earth. And to you and to me. I assume that you, just like me, belong to that 98.5% of people whom I suspect have never seen an angel. What practical help can a book like this be to you? And I think that a book like this is only of some purpose if it can be of practical help. We humans have gone much too far along the path towards some huge disaster to have the time to spare to have a nice conversation about angels.

Are you, dear reader, beginning to suspect that I want to drive the mainly de-Christianised Western world back to the church? Just forget that idea, I am not that silly.

Will not the 98.5% say of a book like this that it is pure speculation? Perhaps hankering after medieval fairy tales, backed up by a few cases from my surgery?

And will all those who have nothing to do with biblical Christianity but feel themselves much more drawn to the eastern religions, not have a much stronger argument in that you never really hear about angels in other religions?

I have an explanation for this last point.

Western civilisation has taken the Judeo-Christian concept of the world as the basis of its belief, which is the belief in one God. As soon as you allow this concept to fall away you see something extraordinary happen. Then you see the hosts of angels take on a different role in popular belief. They move up one grade and become as gods.

And this applies both to fallen angels and the ones that have not fallen. In order not to wander off too far, let us take the old Greek gods as examples, old Zeus with his capricious character and with a taste for fun and games with earthly women. Is not that a clear description of one of the fallen angels about whom we hear in Bible stories? Those who left their heavenly abode and who begot giants by such women (Genesis 6, verses 1 − 4).

That is why I think that the gods of other peoples are the angel princes of Christianity and that the devas of India are the angels of the west. They are given other names, but they are the same beings.

I must add something more to this.

In this world there is a curious principle that undoubtedly has a connection with the influence of angels. It is difficult to put an exact name to this principle, but in practice it works like this: you focus your attention on a particular subject and after a time you receive from the outside world all kinds of facts that enable you to see it more clearly. People spontaneously send you a book that proves relevant, a newspaper which is blown past the bench you are sitting on contains a really interesting article on the subject, a remark in company suddenly enables you to reach new insights.

Thus it happened that a few weeks after I wrote these lines, I received a book as a present. It is called 'Angels', is written by Peter Lamborn Wilson and is beautifully illustrated with pictures of different angel hierarchies.

That book gives a crystal clear illustration of how angels have played an important role amongst all peoples as mediators between heaven and earth. For some time the study of angels was at a standstill due to the influence of the rationalism of the previous century. That study is now apparently once more on the increase. It is connected with the times in which we live. These show us a clear change in human interest, the mysterious aspect of life is important once more.

But, once again, of what use is this? Can you do something with it or is it only something that is nice to know or something a bit out of the ordinary. Then I am of the opinion that there definitely is something practical we can obtain from it.

We live in a time which is different from all other times preceding us in our written history, with the possible exception of the century before the Great Flood. As everybody is gradually beginning to know, we possess the weapons that enable us to eradicate most of the life on this planet. The weapons stand poised on both sides of the Iron and Bamboo Curtains and are awaiting the press of a button from the first fool who wanders along.

That is why many people are in agreement that something must change.

After much searching, more and more people discover that there is but one thing you can try to change in this conspiracy of forces that threaten us, and that is man himself. The hydrogen bombs by themselves do not present the greatest danger; it is the man who does not scruple to use them who does.

That is why since the nineteen-sixties a great many experiments have been carried out to see if man cannot be transformed into a somewhat more useful member of Creation. A group of mostly well-intentioned amateurs have thrown themselves with great enthusiasm into this task and thought up ideas such as sensitivity training, scientology, transcendental meditation and other more or less picturesque branches of group psychology with the idea of making man into a friendly and acquiescent sheep. Gurus offer their followers, clad in orange or not, as the case may be, their own brand of salvation and lead them at times into a spiritual slavery that turns them into enervated victims.

The same happens in politics, as when we see the totally obsolete communist system marching under the banner of liberation from all sorrows.

The peripatetic teacher Krishnamurti also stresses that same change in people, but consciously or unconsciously he limits himself so much to emptying the inside that he leaves a vacuum instead of fulfilment. Krishnamurti is a wonderful man, but not a man with solutions. More a man with dissolutions

Now, in the nineteen-eighties, we can state that we have failed to defuse that time bomb, the human being, and that the danger exists that within the forseeable future there will be fragments of a destroyed planet flying around not only between Mars and Jupiter but also between Venus and Mars, sober reminders of the place where once the azure earth hung.

A tendency which is already clearly visible in some places is the strident call from people for a strong man, which would then make dictatorship on a planetary scale a fact. The planet does not then break into pieces, but humanity is reduced to an ant-heap and that is not its mission. Its earthly task is to produce a community where love reigns. A love encompassing all fellow men and the kingdoms lying below us — the animal kingdom, the kingdoms of plants and of minerals. Its task is brotherhood, and not subjection and domination.

Its heavenly assignment is to return, person by person, to God, to Him who asks us humbly to serve and be warm. And that is, of course, not possible under a dictatorship, for such is ruled by fear.

A dictatorship without terror has never been possible. Dreams of a just dictatorship are about as unrealistic as dreams of a virgin prostitute. A dictatorship on a planetary scale is, seen from a spiritual point of view, an unimaginable disaster.

But if we have proved to ourselves that we cannot cope, and if a world dictatorship is a bad alternative, what then?

Then we can only admit that we need help. And that is the most awkward thing conceited man can do. Suppose that the party wanting to gain votes through the use of slogans had to admit, 'We do not have the faintest idea how we are really to solve it all.' Or that a mighty dictator would say, 'Will somebody in the crowd perhaps tell me if he sees a solution to our problems? I cannot see any way out myself just now.' Or that an important professor in a cancer institute would just for once stop giving out ever more impressive statistics of cure to the world, and simply sigh, 'More and more people are dying!' Can you imagine such a situation? Then you know immediately what is wrong. A man would sooner cut out his tongue than admit that he cannot deal with a problem, and particularly if he is at the top of the ladder of his profession.

And yet we need urgent help from outside because we humans have proved ourselves incapable. Thus we are caught in the dilemma: The human race is rushing to the cliff-edge and needs help in order not to fall off. The leaders of the human race, and therefore their following (and that is us) will not admit that they are incompetent but prefer to claim that, given enough tax money, every problem can be solved.

The catastrophe seems unavoidable.

And opposed to all this is the fact that our heavenly rear guard almost certainly knows very well how we are to solve these problems, and is flooding us with good impulses in order to help us.

In contrast to that are the many bad inspirations that are sent to us, and the human race has a tendency to listen to wicked inspirations because they have always supplied pleasure. Nobody would listen to bad inspirations if they did not feed one or other pleasure centre within us.

Now it is a fact that certain pious communities say, 'If people only hold to the Ten Commandments, then all will be well.' Obviously that is true, and if our society were to be truly based on the Ten Commandments then we would have come a long way. Only, it just is not so. And what is more, we are faced with a number of exceptionally complex problems. Our society has become complicated to such an extent that you cannot solve the practical problems of today using only the Ten Commandments. The Ten Commandments are to be compared with the Constitution, but the execution of these Commandments requires a formulation suitable to this century, which is still largely absent. And that makes for great confusion.

Let me take a concrete example. For many years it was precisely the Protestant part of the Dutch population which showed a strong preference for homoeopathic medicines, since it is these which are taken directly from God's world. In the last five years the tide has turned. Suddenly Dutch Protestants turn up at the surgery and say that they do not want to take the high-potency preparations as these would be occult. Neither do they want medicines made by anthroposophic-based companies because 'anthroposophists sow their plants at particular phases of the moon' and that is a heathen activity. These worthy citizens ignore the fact that they are totally unconcerned when they swallow a preparation of hormones made from the urine of pregnant mares, surely not in accordance with the Mosaic food laws. Or when they take a tranquilliser to calm down their tension when the Bible clearly says, 'Be wakeful!'

Here you can clearly see that the constitution is just, but that there seems to be confusion over the way it is applied in these new times when so much has changed so fundamentally that almost no one can keep up with the tempo.

The Ten Commandments also seem to have little to say when we want to solve the energy crisis, the pollution of our environment, the devaluation of money, and overpopulation, to mention but a few of our present burning questions.

In the Bible there is an elaboration of the Ten Commandments, namely the 248 things that you must do, and the 365 things you must not do, but these do not give any directions

196

for current problems either. They were written with an agrarian rather than an industrial population in mind, and they would need to be translated into the terms of our own times to provide solutions for our problems. But not in the sense of, 'From good Hebrew into good English', but more in the way of an interpretation of dreams.

You remove some of the clothes from a symbol of those times and put on the clothes of these times and it is only then that you can draw a few conclusions. To take an example:

The Mosaic food laws tell us exactly what is clean and what is unclean. But someone who sticks to the letter of that law still runs the risk of contracting typical cultural illnesses if he feeds himself with refined sugar, white bread, canned meat and vegetables, soft drinks with all their artificial colouring and sweeteners, and if he smokes cigarettes (which are not mentioned anywhere in the Bible).

The concepts clean and unclean will thus have to be redefined. Quite good and just in their own terms, but these times require a re-evaluation because we are much more impure than in those ancient times when you have only clean and dirty animals, whereas we have 2000 new and mostly carcinogenic chemicals in our environment.

And then again another strange fact arises. Many Dutch Protestants regard health food stores with great suspicion, while it is precisely here that food is sold of which Moses would have approved. But in health food stores we also often see advertisements for this or that meditation technique, or for some Eastern philosophy (and then they think that from a religious point of view the purity of the food cannot make the grade.

So you come across the strange situation that those who cling most strongly to the Bible are the ones who take their stand with what is least godly, and that those who do not regard the Bible very highly are most often the very ones who recommend techniques, eating habits and medicines that are virtually sanctifying our planet.

The evangelical Protestant buys food for her family that is stiff with insecticides and articifical additives, while many guru-worshippers use their last pennies to buy organically grown food and keep their bodies clean.

It reminds one of those children's books where you can keep on putting different heads on different bodies. The head of the mayor on the body of a clown, the head of a mustachioed policeman on the body of a ballet dancer.

That is why there seems to be a crying need in our times to clearly redefine the values in the three vital areas of spirit, soul and body, and how we can apply these estimations in our society.

A number of these values are of course known, but everything is so incredibly fragmented that no one knows precisely where he is.

A minister of the Dutch Reformed Church once said to me, 'The Reformed Church has grown large with the gin bottle' (after which he poured himself another one). The question now is, with what is the new man to grow large? Whisky? Or fruit juice?

May I repeat a few points:

1. In the world of angels all the help that is needed for people is at hand.
2. That world wants to help us under the leadership of God.
3. New ideas stream towards us, both positive and negative ones.
4. We human beings always have to choose between the streams from above and the streams from below, but we must not imagine that we make these streams ourselves. We are receivers and choosers, not creators.
5. The problems of this world can no longer be solved by ordinary human powers and are leading directly to a catastrophe on a planetary scale.
6. The leaders of humanity, that is the ones holding the

198

reins of power, have no direct intention of taking over in a constructive way to prevent this fatal development. They have ears to hear but do not hear, and eyes but do not see, and they think 'Après moi le deluge . . .'

7. Those people who do not lead, who do not have power, that is you and I, would dearly like to see changes in this situation but lack the ability to do anything about it.

As we look at these seven points it seems that the situation has become stuck, as if it cannot possibly be solved. Yet there are people who have enough room to move to be able to deal with it all. Who are they? These are the people mentioned in point 7. Us, and by that I mean the ordinary, lowly citizen without powers, must ask for help. It is as simple as that.

But how do you carry out such a resolution? I can hardly sit in the middle of a large highway causing a huge traffic jam and then, when the police arrive and ask 'What are you doing here?' answer with, 'I am sitting here asking for help against nuclear armament.' That does not get us anywhere and nuclear armament just carries on.

Let us make a list of ways to contact heaven, from whence we must obtain our help. Assuming, of course, that the need to obtain help is a fact.

I shall not be able to mention all possibilities, but I will do my best to mention a number of them.

A. Prayer

When praying, man acknowledges that he is not his own master, but is a creature who is able to ask its Creator for advice.

A basis of prayer is that it must be clear and well-formulated. Then you see miracles happen time and again. Moreover, you must have the attitude that you do not doubt for a moment that you will be helped. In fact, it should be that you give thanks before seeing the help arrive.

I often ask people about their relationships with others. 'How is your relationship with your husband?' 'How is your relationship with your children?' And then sometimes I ask in the same tone of voice, 'How is your relationship with God?'

Most people look up bewildered. 'What do you mean by that?'

'Well, are you in contact with God?'

Then they say, 'Is that really possible?'

'You could try praying.'

Then many say, 'I used to do that long ago, but I never got any answer. One day I just stopped.'

That is an important problem. I used to think that people who spoke like that really got no answer, but gradually I have come to a totally different conclusion. People think they do not get an answer; it is often that they do not pay attention or even that they forget. Just suppose that you have a problem and you explain the problem as you pray. Do not expect a tailor-made answer. Write down exactly what you asked for, and then go and look at what happens with expectation in your heart. Read your question once more a month later and then it often appears that your problem has been solved. But it all happened so gradually and in such a friendly manner that you totally forgot to be grateful for the solution. You forgot the event.

Answers to prayers often come only some considerable time later and if you are not paying attention you can miss them.

But there are also some of those great tragic problems such as the incurable disease of a loved one or the cooling down of love. And even if a person believes in a miracle with all his power, often such a prayer is not answered. Why does this happen? Are you then not good enough? Or were you unworthy of the trouble, or maybe did you sin too much?

This can lead to great suffering. Pouring your heart out in prayer, explaining your problem, does not mean that the problem will be solved in the way you wanted. You often see that the person whose prayer is not answered gets something else instead. Inexplicable extra support. An inner peace.

'How must I pray?' people ask. And also, 'Surely I cannot bother the great God with something like that?' (As if He would be too busy.)

Well, Christianity has used the Lord's Prayer for some two thousand years. Everyone who does not know how to pray and therefore does not even make a start could learn this prayer.

The Lord's Prayer contains a remarkable clause, 'Forgive us our debts, as we forgive our debtors' (Matthew 6, verse 12). In practice I have often noticed that prayers do not 'want to rise' when people hold a grudge in their heart. Then indeed there is a broken connection with heaven. But when they let go of that grudge, suddenly the connection with God is restored or perhaps comes into existence for the first time.

Actually the whole Lord's Prayer is full of wonders. An explanation would require the writing of a separate book. I would like to point out the strange phrase, 'Lead us not into temptation . . .'

Is that possible? Can God lead man into temptation? Does He not intend the best for us? And yet, I understand a little of that expression. Imagine a man who is totally righteous in his own eyes. He keeps strictly to the Ten Commandments, and does a lot of good besides. But he has one difficulty — he is intolerant towards those who do not adhere so strictly to the Ten Commandments. And as he grows older, his intolerance grows. He bemoans the wickedness of the world, and yes, he even preaches against it with great force. Actually such a man quite understands the Inquisition. And then one day he stumbles.

It could be an affair with another woman, or a break with his parents or some financial trouble, and the beautiful vase is broken. Perhaps nobody knows about it, but the righteous one has fallen, just like any ordinary mortal.

And what do you see happening? After some time such a man becomes mild. He still believes in the Ten Commandments, but he is not exalted above his weak fellow men. Then God has led him into temptation in order to test him in difficult circumstances and to break him.

Thus if you pray, 'Lead me not into temptation,' then you really say, 'Let it not be necessary. Allow me to see the difficulty in time so as to avoid having to learn the lesson in a hard and painful manner.'

Thus, if you have lost the habit, start praying once again and write down what you ask. Our memory is weak in these things. Or, if you have never prayed, start very simply, every day, and see how this gives a certain scent in your life. So that you become nearer to what you were meant to be.

Prayers remind me at times of firework rockets. Such a rocket shoots up and then there comes a star and every point of that star explodes into seven new stars, and with very expensive rockets you see that process repeated once more. So it is with prayers sometimes. You ask something very simple and you get a chain reaction. My prayer influences the life of my son, his life influences seven others and each of those lives influences seven more. And that can go on for years. If you notice such things you will stand there open-mouthed. And then the people who are truly strong in prayer are not so far removed as you might at first think, for it is not the power of our prayer but the might of God who hears them through which miracles happen.

Let me tell you two stories about such miracles:

One of the most famous prayers of this century was that of General Patton. After his great breakthrough in Normandy, the allied armies spread out over Europe and stood at the borders of Germany and as far as Arnhem. But there was a dangerous weak spot in their lines and when it began to snow so badly that the allied air force had to be grounded, the German general Von Rudstedt attacked in the Ardennes, in an attempt to recapture Antwerp. During that Christmas offensive of 1944 the fate of the allied expeditionary force hung by a thread. Everything depended on the weather, but the weather reports remained gloomy.

Then Patton walked into his map room in a furious temper and to the bewilderment of his staff began to speak firmly to God. 'I need four days of fine weather,' he said, 'otherwise I cannot be held responsible for the consequences.' He also had this prayer printed on 300,000 Christmas cards.

The skies broke, the allied air force took off and the German offensive was smothered. Patton did not forget to give hearty thanks to his Lord, again within earshot of his staff, whilst pointing at the map to show how the German offensive had been stopped. The fine weather lasted four days. Was God on the side of the allies? Everyone who has seen photographs of the concentration camps which were discovered when Germany was invaded will not doubt that God chose sides.

A somewhat more domestic example:

Old aunt Corrie ten Boom, an evangelist, was staying with an invalid friend in Florida. There came a warning of one of those hurricanes with the friendly girlish name of Elly or

Freda or some such. After a few further measurements it appeared that the eye of the storm was going to pass directly over the house of her friend. If this happened the house would be sucked up as if through a giant vacuum cleaner.

Aunt Corrie began to pray, and the hurricane hesitantly stood still. She went on praying and the hurricane appeared to shrug its shoulders, turned off to the right and vanished to the north, where it blew itself out over the open sea.

A person who prays in full expectation can thus expect miracles. I have personally seen so many that the power of prayer is no longer a matter of doubt for me.

There have been so many excellent books written on this subject that I will refer the reader, who wants to know more of these. For instance the books of Francis McNutt or Kathryn Kuhlman.

Hans Schroeder says something remarkable on the subject of prayer. He tells that while we pray our guardian angel always prays with us and that he adds, as it were, his own essence to the prayer, which is why it can ascend more easily to God.

Our guardian angel hopes that we pray to God. For the greatest happiness that any angel can hope for is to see clear to the Lord. But because he has to watch us all day long, and we are busy dealing with the world, he has little time to see up to the Lord and that causes him to suffer a great deal.

I cannot prove that all this is true, but I am of the opinion that a person at prayer not only personally receives grace but makes his angel happy.

B.   The Dream

People have another place where they can connect with heaven. This one is much less certain than prayer, much more random, but of great interest nonetheless. It is a place which he enters every night, although not everyone realises this. It is the sphere of dreams.

Everybody dreams five times in a night, whether he remembers it or not. Holland, with its fourteen million inhabitants has thus seventy million dreams a night. An impressive total. That means in a year there are 25,550 million dreams produced in Holland, or a good twenty-five billion.

These dreams are not just personal 'day-trips', no, they often contain very worthwhile indications.

In 1981 I wrote down 168 dreams and when I sorted through this material at the end of the year, fourteen dreams proved to have materialised exactly. One in twelve thus contained a very accurate indication of the future.

This was quite clear in some dreams, even as I wrote them down. Other dreams could only later be recognised as predictions.

Thus I saw a friend with a completely swollen face and one eye closed up. I could not interpret the dream, but that proved afterwards to have been impossible because some months later she looked exactly that way from having a car door slammed against her.

On March 15, 1981, I saw a large wound in my hand from which blood welled up. It was May 2, 1982 when I actually chopped my hand with an axe. The wound was of the same size as in my dream, although it was in a slightly different place.

Sometimes you interpret your dreams symbolically and yet they come out quite differently:

Thus I dreamed on January 30, 1981 that one of us was sailing a yacht and took a wrong turn, into a canal. The boat circled through a lot of duckweed and then drifted through some green stalks and moored against the bank to the right. By way of commentary I wrote down on that same day that the member of my family involved had to manoeuvre carefully when putting together an awkward letter and I was very proud of this clarifying explanation. On July 15 though, this dream actually took place, in Friesland. Only the stalks turned out to be just water plants.

And sometimes a dream can occur at several levels simultaneously:

On March 9, 1981 I dreamed that my mother's house had reached an advanced state of dilapidation. The thatched roof had come off, boards were lying everywhere. I interpreted that as the impending death of my mother and that indeed proved to be the case some three months later. But what I had not expected was that the house turned out to be in a bad condition, and that in 1982 I really saw part of what I had dreamed, to wit, dilapidation and boards everywhere, and that in 1983 I saw the second part of the dream come true, for the roof then had to be renewed.

Sometimes the dream dives into a problem and then surfaces with a crystal clear diagnosis:

Thus I once dreamed that I was holding a fibrous fruit in my hand. I peeled it and saw inside a fine network of ragged red fibres. Then I awoke, and I copied down the fruit as I had seen it very accurately, only to find that I had drawn a womb. A few days later one of my patients was to have a D and C and I was worried because the specialist had suspected a cancer. On the basis of this dream I wrote down immediately that no tumour would be found as the womb looked normal. It all occurred exactly as I had predicted.

From these dreams we can see that much that is true, even about our everyday lives, is contained in dreams. A huge potential lies in dreams, but it is not often tapped except on the psychoanalyst's couch.

The area in which we find ourselves during our dreams is not as private as we might think. Thus the Brain-Mind Bulletin of September 13, 1982 mentions the following:

In Virginia, USA, a group of people carried out an experiment in dreaming with extra ordinary results. The participants agreed that they would meet one another in the dream world under particular circumstances. Amongst the participants were a student, a professor of mathematics, a minister, someone doing technical medical work, etc.

'In one of our dreams we met each other in a bus,' recounts one of the members of the group. 'Almost everyone turned up.' But the strange thing was that the other ten members of the group confirmed this and one had even made a cartoon of the event. It may be a shock to some people that another person can remember your dream, and yet it may be possible.

Dreams can thus be influenced by the decisions that you make before going to sleep, and besides this you can act together with another person in your dream.

The group in the United States was made up in such a fashion that one half of the participants were ordinary dreamers, and the other half lucid dreamers. Ann Faraday has written about this phenomenon in her exceptionally good books on dreams. It is difficult to explain to someone who has not experienced this for himself, but a lucid dream is one in which the sleeper does not experience the dream unconsciously but keeps a very clear consciousness and thus retains the freedom to act. I shall try to explain all this by means of an example. I dreamt that I was flying over a large road. I fly a lot in my dreams, so that was nothing special. I knew the road well, it is not far from my home, with a wood to the right and pastures to the left that end at the foot of the dunes.

208

An enormous ancient arch of eroded yellow stone had been built over the road. There was an inscription in old Greek letters on it. Suddenly I glanced at my hands and I realised that I was dreaming. And from that moment I was totally awake in my dream. I could go wherever I wanted, I saw the colours much more intensely and clearly than in my waking life and I knew all the time that I was dreaming and that I was free within my dream. It was much later that I read in the books of Castaneda that an old Indian shaman gave him the advice to try to look at his hands when dreaming, since that is how you gain lucidity.

The experience of a lucid dream is somewhat extraordinary. You feel completely intelligible, happy and free from the heaviness of the body. Through your thinking, you have an enormous influence on your surroundings. Thus I tried to prove to myself that I was indeed dreaming, and I lengthened my arm to pick up something standing in the middle of a pond. When I had picked it up I said triumphantly, 'You see, I really am dreaming.' For of course it is not possible to lengthen an arm in real life.

I understand that Freudians will immediately explain the dream in sexual terms, but that does not detract in any way from the fact that I was completely lucid and consciously 'present'; more conscious than I usually am during the day.

It is mentioned in Peter Lamborn Wilson's book 'Angels' that every man has an invisible doppelganger, a sort of heavenly twin. It is the angel which you could become and with which — if you are to belong to the heavenly company — you will become united after your death. During lucid dreams this unity with the heavenly double exists for a short time, and is a wonderful experience.

Now I could imagine that, just as people pray together, those people who have lucid dreams should agree to take a given problem with them into their dream. Such a dream group would compare solutions afterwards and I am convinced that very original discoveries would come out of this. Heaven is delighted to help us and the only requirement given is that we make clear contact.

It is important that when a person is given a task either in prayer or in a dream, he should carry out that task. A sort of circulation of the blood is set up with heaven. You ask for guidance, then you get an answer, you carry out the suggestion, and you get further support when carrying out the task. Listening but not carrying out blocks the channels.

When doing these things it is important to observe certain criteria:

1. Check that the errand comes from heaven.
2. Ensure that the errand is carried out in such a way that the original good inspiration is not spoiled by bad impulses so as to be pushed gradually to its opposite.

   The first point may be recognised by the following:

All messages from heaven are designed to increase the love towards God and the love for other people. Thus they will never urge a love of domination or interference. The hellish spirits, who can mix evil inspiration with the good, are often very crafty. They wrap their love of domination in such beautiful-sounding slogans that even the best of us are fooled.

As far as the second point is concerned, I will give the following example because it is typical of its kind:

In the 1930s there lived (and still lives!) in Vlaardingen a general practitioner called Cornelius Moerman. This man had a brand-new idea about the treatment of cancer. He thought that cancer was not a localised disease, but a total degeneration of the metabolism, and thus he tried to cure cancer with a special diet that included vitamins and minerals. His endeavours met with immediate success and within a very short time cancer patients from all over the place came to Moerman to be cured.

The official medical world was not at all pleased and Moerman faced trial after trial, but being one of those indestructible men from staunch Dutch farming stock he weathered all storms and people continued to flock to his surgery.

An official committee from the Department of Health looked into Moerman's work and said that it was nonsense. Moerman offered to drive his pitchfork as a spit into the chairman of the committee. Then, after more than forty years of persevering alone, suddenly a group of Dutch medical doctors combined their efforts and began to follow the methods of Dr Moerman. This happened in the mid-nineteen-seventies. It appeared that Moerman's methods could indeed cure cancer patients and soon the other twenty-five doctors were also deluged with cases. The word got around and the Department of Health became severely worried. New trials against these 'Moerman doctors' only helped to make them more popular and a large association of cancer victims sprang up to help these doctors against the repressive measures of the Government.

Eventually a member of the equivalent of the House of Commons proposed to initiate research that would evaluate the non-toxic treatment of Dr Moerman. In 1979, the vote was passed by the House with a comfortable majority.

Now watch what happened. Here is a group of twenty-five doctors using the 'gentle' cancer treatment in their practices. And here is a vote in the House of Representatives that this method should be looked into, if only because if it was of any value then patients' expenses could be refunded by the Dutch medical welfare scheme.

Then for two years nothing happened. During those two years a state committee met regularly to think about this research. These meetings were very expensive. In them there was nobody to represent the doctors who practised the Moerman-method. Not once did the committee try to make contact with these doctors. And then after two-and-a-half years suddenly all the doctors practising Moerman therapy received some sort of book. In it were laid down the regulations governing research into the Moerman methods and the letter accompanying the book more or less ordered the doctors to start straight away with the research. During that time I was the secretary of the 'Moerman doctors' and I asked the State officials who they really thought they were. A row lasting for another two-and-a-half years followed this friendly question.

The book, referred to as the research protocol, changed its tune three times and during all that time still not one of the doctors offering non-toxic cancer treatment had a word to say about its contents.

And then finally came a result. The Department of Health expected the 'Moerman doctors' to be happy with it and to start the research. A big grant has been promised.

When you look into this research programme, it is one of the biggest scandals in Dutch medical history. It is like the silk cord that the Japanese emperor sent to those of his opponents whom he wanted removed.

'Here, go and hang yourself.'

It all looks very fair and above board until you come to the 'selection of the patients'. Then you see that only those patients are selected who 'have been treated with all the possibilities of orthodox cancer treatment and yet during the last three months show further deterioration'.

In practice these are the terminal patients.

There is another group of patients who 'have received no treatment other than an operation, whose health has deteriorated further during the last three months, and who have received no further treatment during those three months'. This group is virtually non-existent.

And, a most amazing and humiliating fact: there is to be no control group. There will also be no 'blind' checks which means that the orthodox cancer specialists who are hostile to the non-toxic methods will always know that 'here is

212

another of these patients who had been treated with this hateful method'. This makes for enormous bias and no hope of objectivity.

Officials from one of our big universities have called this research programme a 'thoroughly bad piece of work'.

So what do we see here? A good impulse (research into non-toxic cancer treatment) is twisted out of context and made into a weapon to prove that non-toxic cancer treatment is a swindle. For as you can see for yourself: When you have two groups of patients, one made up of the terminally ill and the other practically non-existent, the results can only be detrimental to the method you wish to test.

The doctors using non-toxic cancer treatment have, of course, refused all co-operation with this plan.

I give you this example because it is so typical of the disturbance which always appears in this world when a good impulse is born. Then the dragon always lies in wait to devour it. That does not matter, as long as we know about it. For then we can take care that not only is the impulse born but that it grows up. Fruitful ideas infect a wide surrounding area in a positive manner and trickle into the way of thinking and behaviour of a whole community.

This phenomenon has been very effectively described by Ken Keyes in his book 'The Hundredth Monkey'. A number of scientific researchers introduced a sweet potato into a community of monkeys living on the isle of Koshima. They threw the potato into the sand in front of the monkeys and watched to see what happened. The monkeys liked the potato, but did not like the sand which clung to the potato. Then a female monkey discovered that she could wash the potato in a brook. For that you have to be a woman. She taught the trick to the community immediately around her and now they have two types of ape: in her immediate vicinity the properly behaved monkeys eat washed potatoes, the others eat sand-covered potatoes. But gradually the habit started to spread. At a certain moment a critical point is reached because literally within one day there is a quantum leap in the monkey culture and that evening the whole monkey community washed its potatoes. Thus we see the gradual build-up from first one female monkey to a hundred monkeys and then suddenly the leap from a hundred monkeys to all the monkeys of the tribe. The period of the slow curve lasted many months, the period of the fast break lasted one single day.

But then something totally unexpected happens: the habit is taken over completely, spontaneously and without visible contact by monkey communities living on other islands.

Apparently, if it has penetrated into enough heads, an idea can become common knowledge. That is why you must never doubt that when you start you have to work up slowly to the critical point.

In this connection the revolutionary book of Rupert Sheldrake, 'A New Science of Life' may be of importance.

He says that if something new comes into existence on this earth, it builds up a 'thought form' and that in this way the new idea penetrates more and more easily. A simple example:

The first Dutchman who learned to cycle built up what could be called a 'bicycle field', so that each following generation could learn to cycle more easily. Not only the Dutch, but also, for instance, an inland African tribe who have never seen a bicycle.

Positive infection via what are called 'fields' (or, more fully, morphogenic fields, i.e. form-creating fields) have begun to be seen as a serious possibility here and there ever since Sheldrake's book. This gives rise to a completely new theory of evolution.

Those fields do not come from us. All creativity is first depositied within us. Steiner says that one of the tasks of the hierarchy of guardian angels is to deposit fertile images into our souls.

If therefore you have received a positive impulse in your dreams or while you were praying, and have passed in on, who knows how far it will carry?

C. Meditation

Just as a great deal has been published on the subjects of prayer and dreams, much has also been written about meditation. My intention here is not to add to it, but merely to attempt to set something straight.

I have noticed that the religiously orthodox often look askance at meditation. They see a strange eastern penetration into western patterns of belief.

On the other hand you see those practising meditation often looking down on those who pray, simply because they regard meditation as a higher form of prayer.

This is not true. We are looking at two entirely different things.

Prayer is the conscious search for contact with God. Meditation is a matter of bringing the mind to stillness. In meditation a person is like a tortoise that pulls in its head and legs. The five senses are at rest. 'Sitting still, doing nothing' is the Zen description of meditation.

During prayer one directs praise, gratitude and supplication at the Creator. Meditation brings your awareness to the level of a higher world. Prayer allows you to speak with Him Who lives there. Bringing the mind to a state of rest through meditation can thus be supportive to prayer.

A remarkable side-branch of meditation is conscious visualisation as used in medical treatment. A lively visualisation of a healing process that can promote the cure, or even of an internal guide who gives advice.

This is visualised as an old man on a mountain meadow and is really present to many people possessing a strong imagination and often gives very detailed advice. The advice can be so original that the querist often says, 'Why didn't I think of that before?'

It also appears that while in the meditative state, we often find solutions to the important problems of our life. Either the problem loses its importance, or an original solution comes 'out of the blue'.

Thus, meditation is one of the most important ways of clearing the channel to the above. Meditation does not mean thinking about something, though it is often used in that sense. No, it is the opening up of the right half of the brain, the directing of the radar aerial at heaven.

It is remarkable to what extent contemporary man has lost the ability to realise that he has an inner world as well as an outer one. That has more or less always been the case, but during this century he has exceeded all records as regards this.

Perhaps someone will say, 'But surely I know what I feel, I notice what I think!' At least I get that answer frequently when I say to people that they are not aware of themselves. And then I ask in return, 'Are you sure?' To give an example: I am filled with a feeling of disappointment. I had expected approval, consideration and respect from someone and he treats me as if I am an ordinary little man, then I feel as if I have been short-changed.

I will find the person who does a thing like that to me unsympathetic and I will even try to do him a bad turn if I get the opportunity. But all this is not conscious, it is purely a feeling that possesses me. At that moment I AM that frustration.

But now imagine that I bring my senses to a stand-still, that I withdraw them from the outer world, withdraw from the person who has short-changed me. Then I can calmly observe the frustration lying inside me, as if I am another person looking at myself. Only, the other person looking at myself is much more 'me' than the one with all the frustrations.

To the feeling of pure frustration you add the sunbeam of consciousness and then that sensation is not going to remain.

218

If you keep looking calmly and objectively, then that negative feeling begins to evaporate like a haze under the rays of the sun.

Thus, there is a great difference between having an inner world and being conscious of that inner world. If you only have it, then you ascribe that inner world to the outer world and then you are insulted, disappointed, wild, frenetic, fanatic, etc. etc. But if you deliberately allow light into your inner world, then you add a new dimension to your life, and then you really start living.

Well now, that is what meditation is all about.

Prayer, dreams and meditation can direct the very much externalised twentieth century man inwards and help him find a way towards the worlds from which help streams. It is best not to do that by yourself, building up a regular discipline is much easier if done in a group where the members stimulate each other. A prayer circle, a dream club, a mediation group or perhaps even a combination of all three.

From such a group a beneficial influence emanates over a wide area. It probably does more to foster world peace than a demonstration with banners. For salt added to food gives a more intensive result than milk that has boiled over.

Therefore I plead for the setting up of many small like-minded groups who consciously want to contact heaven. The angels await them.

The difficulty is that the whole communist leadership as well as the majority of western technocrats have no ties with heaven and therefore lay themselves wide open to evil influences from hell. The result can be seen all around us these days. Let me keep to just one example.

Nowadays there is a flurry of activity around test tube babies. Of course it is a little unfortunate that quite a few embryos are left over and it would be a pity to just dump them. That is wasteful. Surely you can make better use of them in interesting experiments?

How long can you keep them alive? Can a baby grow to term outside the womb? How does it react to pain?

And everybody must by now have come to the realisation that experiments are also carried out on those embryos that become avaliable through abortion and which did not have the sense to die immediately.

Take note, that is hell at work. It is the expert, the technocrat, who has sold his soul to the devil and that happens all too easily. Everything in the name of a science without conscience. And against this there are no loud protests. Do you hear it talked about in church? Is there one single church which threatens excommunication to its members who co-operate even remotely with these practices?

There is still no clear answer to the dehumanisation of our age. There has been, here and there, in small groups, but it needs to be stated louder and more clearly.

If many more people put themselves out for this then a new elite would be set up. I know that this is something of a dirty word today, for elite usually indicates money, power and family and that is still the case in many countries, especially in those ruled by a dictator. But I do not mean that sort of elite.

It needs to be an elite made up out of people who radically reject the exercise of power. People who are prepared to work co-operatively with heaven for the good of this planet. A certain amount of selection has to take place, but this is simple. The new elite will be judged by the question, 'Do you belong to heaven or hell?'

However, then we must define heaven and hell carefully, otherwise you start almost immediatley with mutual heresy and the game goes back right to where it started. Heaven is connected to everything that makes this planet and its inhabitants cleaner, happier and healthier. Hell is connected with everything that makes it dirtier, less happy and more enslaved. Of course, evil inspiration will do everything to sow dissent within members of the group.

It is a good idea to go a little further into what could possibly happen to a group of people who try to connect more closely with heaven. If false information is recognised and an attempt to divide the group does not succeed, is that group home and dry? In no way, for then the attack comes from outside. Let us imagine that there is a group who has received an impulse direct from heaven and who now wants to try to realise this impulse here on earth. What happens to it? First, people try to hush it all up, but if that does not work they try to ridicule it. Then if that does not get any results, the cry 'unscientific' goes up. And if all that has no effect, the real attack is la͏͏ ͏ ͏ned, usually disguised behind a mask of grandiloquence.

All this happens wherever people bring innovative ideas. I have been talking here about meditation and prayer groups but I could have been talking about any group of people who are really and honestly concerned, without ulterior motives, about the destiny of this planet and the human race, and who want to do something about it.

Again, allow me to take an actual example:

The more you think about this planet, the more you come to the conclusion that it is not just a piece of rock covered with plant life that spins in empty space. After careful observation you get the feeling that it is a living entity. Of course it is not built like us, but nonetheless it has a life of its own. When we talk about the great rain forests then we are really talking about the 'green lungs' of this planet. And we talk about the great water arteries. And really, if you fly over the world then you see quite clearly that the rivers are living arteries. The earth breathes, has blood circulation and its own body temperature.

Think of the ebb and flow of the tides. Are those not perfect examples of a living planet? Yes, I know perfectly well that it has now been discovered that these tides are affected by the moon but that is a typically materialistic explanation which leaves you suspended in the middle of nowhere. It is nice to know, but you lose your sense of wonder.

The sea lies there, breathing like some gigantic animal. Breathing in for six hours when the tide rises, then breathing out for six hours so the tide recedes. We are used to this here, but take a look in Britanny, France. One moment the sea lies stretched out beyond endless beaches with here and there a small hillock, and then you see the flood come rolling towards you from the distance. It creeps across those miles of beach and a few hours later there is nothing left of those sandy shores, just here and there a few islands stick up out of the water.

What kind of mighty movement is that? And if everything that we can perceive with our senses has, apart from a material meaning, also a deeper significance, what is then the inner sense of that movement? We are thus dealing with the phenomenon of a rhythmic rising and falling of the water level. Some time ago I stood with my wife looking at the great locks at Ijmuiden. A tanker from Panama was being moved through the locks. It was ebbing, and after the gates were shut on the seaward side the ship had to rise for some considerable time so as to reach the higher level of the North Sea Canal and thus be able to continue its journey to Amsterdam.

And while I stood calmly watching I suddenly realised that this event was a perfect image of the ebb and flow in our awareness.

When we wake up in the morning, we crawl as it were from out of the great sea of the subconscious onto land. Our diurnal awareness awakes. Our ship begins to travel along a canal at the elevated level of the surrounding countryside. We have passed up through the lock, but that did not take place abruptly. There is always a transitional period between sleeping and waking and then we sit in a sort of psychic lock.

In the evening the ship passes back through the locks and so down to the sea, and so after another transitional period we fall asleep. The various water levels symbolise the various levels of awareness.

It is a good job there are locks in Ijmuiden. Just imagine if there were none, then the low-lying country would be flooded at high tide. We also find this image within man. There are people who have something wrong with their lock, or maybe where the lock is absent. These people are overrun by the contents of their subconscious, and we call these people mad. There are also people whose living awareness has withdrawn too far. The land lies dry and salty under an unfriendly sun. They are continually aware of themselves in a negative manner. This we call depression.

But not only can we perceive in ourselves the important rhythms of day and night. In daytime there are also continuous changes in levels of consciousness. Our awareness is not a rigid, continuous surface but streams flowing to and fro, clear one moment and dull the next, one second cheerful and the next serious.

And now look at the earth as one great organism, as a living being.

Look at those rising and falling water levels that continually release and swallow the land. Will that planet also have an oscillating consciousness, just like us? Can we see that oscillation externally as the movement of ebb and flow?

These are just playful images that I set down, but they allow the reader to participate a little in the living part of our planet.

Thus I sometimes imagine when I walk through a bare forest in winter, that I am a microscopic creature and that the trees I see silhouetted against the wintry sky are the hairs on the skin of the earth.

And to come back once more to the oceans, are they not incredible fountains of life. They are thick with life. Very small life, such as beautiful little coral fish and whimsical plankton, and life that is almost as intelligent as we are, such as whales and dolphins.

Most people do not think very often of the living seas but there is a small group of people who really love the seas of this world. These are the people of Greenpeace. With their small boats they run in front of the large ships that are about to poison the seas with atomic waste products. Or they try to defend their brothers, the seals and whales, and are then imprisoned because they try to take photographs of the slaughter of these friendly animals.

These Greenpeace people do not gain financially, nor do they serve either political nor commercial ends, but they end up with a lot of trouble. But apparently they are such a close unit that they cannot be infiltrated by their enemies and apparently they have kept their enthusiasm, despite all their disappointments. And so what happens next?

Brute force is used, their ship chained down, and people imprisoned.

And then you sometimes see the miraculous when they persevere and break down the opposition with their moral superiority. People armed with only enthusiasm and film cameras break the morale of people armed with helicopters and machine guns.

You can almost imagine the sigh of relief from our planet, that there is still someone who defends it. Perhaps every planet also has an angel to guard it and who says at that instant, 'Greenpeace people, I have come to help you. I love my seas, my seals, and whales. And now I shall support you because you dare to challenge the might of the exploiters. I shall help you break the morale of the enemy.'

Are there indications that such a planetary angel exists? Purely intuitively I would say that it is the female figure seen every now and then and who even in this century has arranged miracles such as those of Fatima.

I do not know in which hierarchy such an angel belongs. Perhaps one of my readers knows. But I do know that the evil attacking small people of good will from the outside often rebounds on the attacker in a miraculous manner. In a way which cannot be explained logically.

The dragon is always ready to devour new impulses. Yes, you can even ask yourself, 'If the dragon is not attacking, am I on the right path?'

Light from heaven causes shadows to be cast on earth. Whoever does not know this gets discouraged.

However, never think that we can do it by ourselves. We must fetch help from where help has always come, from heaven.

It will prove impossible to use materialism to fight materialism. That is pitting force against force, such as SS20 rockets against cruise missiles, that is ever worsening the dehumanisation. Only with heavenly inspiration is help and deliverance possible.

I must now concentrate on an idea which lives, as much in America as in Europe, in the minds of many groups of Christians. This idea is as follows: we live at the end of time forecast by all the prophets. Suppression, persecution and terror will greatly increase. Famine, epidemics and wars will become more severe. Earthquakes will follow each other at an increasing pace. We are not even spared atomic war. One of the cruelest dictators in the history of the world will present himself as the Prince of Peace and seize power over this planet and murder many people. Then, when things cannot get any worse, Jesus Christ comes, and sets up an absolute theocratic power centred on Jerusalem. The oppression is past and the enemies of humanity are guarded against with an iron fist and a thousand years of peace will reign.

Many books have been written about this programme and Hal Lindsey is one of the best-known writers on the subject. These writers base their ideas on biblical prophecies, on the prophetic discourses of Jesus in the Book of Revelations. And really one is saying, 'This is fighting a losing battle. We shall turn up our collars and try to get through the oppression as well as we can till the Lord returns.'

There is a separate group of these Christians who think that they will be taken up to heaven before the great oppression starts so that they can watch the struggles of the remainder from above. And they think to prove this from other biblical prophecies.

I think that, speaking in purely human terms, some danger lies in this reasoning. It tends, as does the eastern concept of reincarnation, to make people passive in the face of current circumstances.

One group says, 'When the Lord returns, He will clean up all the mess.'

The other group says, 'I did not succeed in that during this lifetime so I will use another lifetime for it.'

I do not want to judge which of the prophecies mentioned above may or may not be right. If you look around you will see the disturbing signs that indicate that a number of prophecies are coming true in our lifetime. I only want to point out the effect this attitude has on people. Sometimes it is such that people say, 'Let us bring as many people as possible to the Lord, before darkness falls. The cleansing of the earth must be left to Him.' This is really the old idea of the Church, that the winning of souls is more important than life on this earth.

Let us for a moment imagine that the Queen came to visit you. Her secretary phones and you hear that she plans to come for dinner sometime next week.

What would you do? That is, what practical things would you do?

Well, I think that you would spring-clean your home, and the new dining-room table you dreamed of for so long, is now actually bought. The peeled paint on the window frame in the dining room would get a coat or two of new enamel. Then your wife would go out and buy the dress she had been tempted by for so long. Also the children, to their horror, would be drilled in table manners and even sent to the hairdresser.

In short, that one telephone call would cause a wave of activity in order to receive the Queen as well as possible. Perhaps somebody says, 'I don't care about the Queen.' Then choose someone else whom you admire greatly. Paul Newman, Billy Graham or Mick Jagger.

It does not matter who, as long it is someone who makes you feel honoured that they should visit your home. It matters that you feel, 'He is coming. He is coming personally! He is coming personally to visit me!'

If these large groups of Christians think that their King is coming, why do they not go out and fight to get their home clean? Why are they not the ones who fight against polluting energy, bad agricultural practices, and a poor food industry? For this planet is our home and it is so dirty that the smell rises for miles. Hygiene of the soul is not enough, we must co-operate to make this earth really clean.

What the Christians with their Messianic expectations are saying just now is, 'Be cheerful and do not be afraid. When the Lord comes he will clean up your home.'

Is that the way to treat a King? Surely that is just not done? Not a single Messianic expectation excuses us from the duty to do our utmost to get things sorted out. That we ask help from a heavenly clean-up squad is permitted. But it is not permitted that we sit with our hands folded on our laps and wait to see it all done for us.

But now that Messianic expectation itself. In the year 1000 it also ruled the thoughts of many Christians. People then anxiously awaited the end of the world.

We have nearly arrived at the year 2000 and with slightly more reason than before many people once again expect the end of the world and the return of Jesus Christ.

Is there any reason to think that He, of whom all angel hierarchies are only the humble servants, is on His way back?

While writing this book somebody made me a present of a wonderful book, the second that came falling 'out of the blue'. This book came from Sweden. The German version is called 'Sie erlebten Christus' (or 'They experienced Christ') and is written by Hillerdal and Gustafsson.

These two theologians put an advertisement in a large Stockholm paper asking people if they had met Christ in their lifetime. This advertisement was placed on December 24, 1972.

A flood of letters resulted and from this it appeared that many people had indeed experienced the risen Lord in their own lifetimes.

The parallels with my own research are striking. It concerns ordinary people, men and women, who often had experienced this extraordinary encounter at some time of physical or spiritual need. This meeting had totally changed their lives and attitudes. And yet many had never told of it to another person. They had kept it carefully to themselves, out of fear of being considered insane.

If you read a book like this and then compare it with your own researches, you may well ask yourself what is going on. Would a similar piece of research, if carried out a hundred years ago, have given the same results?

I do not think so. You only have to read the literature of the previous century to see what a totally different atmosphere prevailed.

It was of course a time of fantastic ideas, as was shown by Jules Verne, but more in the sense of unbelievable achievements of man as realised by advancing technological ingenuity. I really think that at present something entirely different is happening and I hope to deal with that in the next chapter.

One thing is really important if you want to be a bridge between heaven and earth, and that is that you must keep both feet on the ground. Otherwise strange things can happen. Some years ago a missionary stayed with one of his colleagues in Africa. One morning he woke early in the still silent house and suddenly heard an extraordinarily penetrating voice say, 'Pray for the peace of Jerusalem.'

The pious man had never before heard a voice from heaven and was deeply touched to receive such a direct assignment. He got out of bed, knelt down and prayed ardently for peace in Jerusalem.

That morning at breakfast he joyfully told his host that for the first time in his life he had heard a voice direct from heaven. His host asked him for the content of the message and when he learned what it was he pulled back a curtain to a conservatory immediately below the bedroom of his guest. There, in a large cage, sat an old parrot who looked wisely at the two gentlemen with his head cocked to one side and then said, 'Pray for the peace of Jerusalem.'

What I want to get across is that when you receive a communication from heaven you must not lose your common sense.

This missionary was the victim of a parrot but you can easily become a victim of yourself. There are endless variations of possible ways of fooling yourself. You ask a question and then the answer you want to hear comes. Watch out, for if heaven has a message it is usually either so original that you would not have arrived at such a conclusion yourself, or it is so unpleasant that you would rather not have heard it. Then you have to do something that you know in your heart of hearts is right but that in real life is the last thing you would like to do.

Clairvoyants of the somewhat baser type often have a tendency to tune in to the daydreams of their client. They then pass these on as a 'message' from a higher being of light to the client who, after payment of a high fee, goes home cheerful.

Thus I knew a couple of which the husband was a Roman Catholic and the wife Protestant. Through the lifetime of their marriage this difference weighed heavily upon them. Finally the husband died and less than two months later the woman came in smiling to tell me that her husband had come through at a spiritualist seance and had told her that her religious ideas were the right ones. Occasions like that are when you can see that people want to be fooled.

Traps and pitfalls also await you when you try to hear the 'still small voice' within. But just imagine that you say, 'When I pray I hear nothing, I never dream and when I try to meditate my mind jumps around like a restless bird from branch to branch.'

For you especially it should prove easy to meet heaven and the angels, for the supernatural can also be experienced on this earth. Look at the clouds, and sometimes you will see a mysterious deep porch opening up. You are then looking into a cave of deep blue, orange and yellow colours. Incredible that you see such a thing, a touch of the heavenly gates.

Listen to the birds, for in the sound of a thrush singing in the spring rain you hear the echo of the angels.

Sometimes you can feel heaven as you listen to the story that your finger tips tell you as you stroke the hair of a small child.

One of the most supernatural things on our planet are the scents of nature. Everyone knows that with the sense of smell one is able to recall long-forgotten memories in a way no other sense can. It is a very subtle sense that really takes in the invisible world. It was not for nothing that people used to talk of spirits of salt (hydrochloric acid), spirit of wine (alcohol) and such like. When we use our sense of smell we directly take in a part of a spirit.

What do we really smell? I think at times we take in the perfume of the angel hierarchies themselves. For scents are also ordered. It must be clear to everyone that the smell of a dog's faeces stands at a lower level than the scent of a rose. They are worlds apart but it seems to me that fragrant scents are also ordered.

Take for instance the musical scale. From C to a higher tone the intervening tones rise from low to high.

Or take the colours of the spectrum. The slow vibrations of red pass into the faster ones of yellow and the very fast ones of blue. Here once again you can talk of a rising octave.

With scents this is more difficult to determine because we cannot, as with tones and colours, express this in terms of so many vibrations per second. You have to go by your feelings and that can, of course, be coloured subjectively. But let me try it nonetheless.

A summer day in the dunes. A very special scent drifts on the breeze. The warm herbal scent of thyme. It seems to invite you to lie down comfortably and doze a little. It is as if the thyme itself seems to hug the earth. Or take the scent of lavender that we know so well from the sun-drenched slopes of southern France. When you take in that scent something warm and cheerful seems to spring up inside you. The scent invites you to wander through nature.

Lavender and thyme are for me intensively connected with the ground, and they make me love the earth. Thyme helps to dissolve the slime of the earth when used in a cough mixture. Lavender drunk in tea helps you to sleep more deeply. These are plants with heavenly smells that lie nonetheless close to the earth.

If you think about it, those scents must surely come from the first heaven. Perhaps every archangel has his own delightful scent of balsam.

Is that why aromatherapy — remedies made from etheric plant oils — gives such tremendous results? Because the oils transfer the health of heaven direct to the earth?

How friendly and healing is the scent of the buds of the North American poplar which I encounter so frequently in the dunes. It is a spring scent. It does not have the languid warmth of summer but spurs you to activity. You breathe more deeply, your strides lengthen, and your head is lifted, it is as if you wake up from hibernation and new creative energy flows into you.

That is certainly a 'higher' feeling than you get from thyme or lavender. Perhaps this is the scent of the kuriotetes, the angels of mercy. Resin is very special. Bees use it to make a substance called propolis or bee-glue which they use to close up their hives, and gaps and holes are sealed up, or predatory insects are embalmed. People, however, use it as a medicine and then at times you see miracles take place. I have even known people suffering from multiple sclerosis improve in health with this substance. This must be a sign that a mighty creative angel is hidden behind the balmy scent of resin.

Let us take jasmine. One moment a green tree which does not look all that special stands in your garden, the next moment there it is in full bridal glory, getting more beautiful every day. Finally, just when you think, 'It can't get any more lovely, it is already so beautiful that it is beginning to hurt', the next day it does get even more gorgeous till a dazzling white flowered veil covers the green. No-one remains unmoved. Even the crabbiest old fossil stops and, as he shakes his head (after all, he approaches everything with disapproval) he says, 'It looks quite nice.'

But the nicest thing is the people visiting my surgery. They have yellow noses because they have stopped briefly to sniff at the pollen-laden flowers.

'It's about time that tree was pruned', says my wife, but I keep putting it off.

The scent of jasmine is one of the most delicate scents that I know.

If you breathe in deeply you will not smell it. You have to take it in gently, just as if you were planning not to smell, and then your whole being is suffused by an indescribable longing, a whiff of eternity. Do we then for an instant smell a little of the 'world in God's shadow'? Did a seraph flutter past?

It would be nice to arrange flower scents in accordance with the angels associated with them. I think in the olden days they were much more advanced in this. People were then consciously using scents to open the mind to higher regions. Thus it is quite noticeable that the Hebrew words of 'spirit' and 'scent' were almost the same — 'ruach' and 'reach'.

It used to be self-evident that the spiritual world (and that of the angels) was coupled to that of scents, but unfortunately nowadays it seems to have left our consciousness. We do not think at all that what we smell could well be something special.

'Just take in the smell', we say of a hyacinth. Or, 'Mmm, just smell this lilac.' But now just imagine that we are really smelling angels. That just as the moon reflects sunlight, so flowers and plants reflect the air of the angels. Then we could be standing on a summer's day in a hollow amongst the dunes smelling the thyme and say, 'Stop a moment, be quiet a second, I smell the angel Uriel!' (Uriel because he is the angel of the east and it is the east wind which heats up our Dutch summers.) Or we could be in Aix-en-Provence, far in the south of France, and smell the scent of the lavender fields and say, 'Michael is very close to the earth today.'

Perhaps you think this is a little fanciful, but it was not all that long ago that people thought that nature was populated by good spirits.

It is terrible that we have lost our ability to perceive their presence because that is why we have lost our respect for this earth and we see our environment solely as something out of which we must extract as much as possible. We do not look into nature, but at nature, as if we are looking at a movie screen. Our world has become two-dimensional, we are the inhabitants of Flatland.

But in reality those deeper dimensions, the angel hierarchies, pass continually through our observations.

What I am talking about here is not nostalgia for a time that will never return. It is a prophecy for a time which is nigh. The power of materialism has almost been broken. Heaven is about to break through, as a pregnant woman feeling the first birth pains. The people will wake up as from a dream and where an age-old sequoia redwood tree stood they will see the self-same tree, but ophanim will be climbing up and down the branches.

Their spiritual ear will hear the rustling of the west wind with the music of angelic choirs led by Raphael, the healing angel from the west. And they will be almost fainting with joy when they know their own prince of angels from nearby, when he has made himself known by the scent of mimosa. If we perhaps experience angels as the scent of flowers, for God it is exactly the other way round. God really experiences the deeds of the person who lives rightly as a sweet fragrance. A person makes a genuine sacrifice so as to help another and God sniffs deeply and says, 'What a fragrant deed I am smelling.' Here we smell perhaps sweat or blood, but in the heavenly regions a fragrant scent of flowers is wafted. Thus we are urged by the scent of jasmine or lilac to become a fragrant scent in heaven ourselves in order that not everything will come from just one side and the balance is readjusted.

Again, man has a choice. Oranges or lemons, what will you choose?

What would you prefer to be, a toadstool or a rose? Choose, it is still possible, it is never too late, not even on your deathbed.

That is what is so special about our earth. The choice remains till the last moment. Literally, right up to our last breath. We live in a world of mercy. A world in which the scent of jasmine rises up to the heavens just as a truck driving past fills your garden with exhaust fumes.

We live in a world which decks itself in a bridal veil each summer to await the arrival of the groom. And we human beings are not simply fertilizer on the fields of the future. The immature communist who made this remark must have been in a particularly bad mood when he penned that thought. No, we are wedding guests, merry party-goers in a profusion of perfumes, cheerful people in a flower carnival of blossoming trees and plants.

How can we prepare for this new world? By becoming a little festive already and mixing our praises with the scent of honeysuckle and lime blossom on a moonlit summer evening.

7. On a Collision Course with Heaven

There may be people who after reading the last chapter feel that I am advocating that you should all switch off your intelligence and live entirely intuitively. But that is not so. I have noticed, for instance, that much psychic energy is lost in vague daydreams. Think of the film Walter Mitty, where the hero is constantly seeing himself in his daydreams in all sorts of heroic situations. It made a nice film, but looked at objectively such a life of daydreams does not lead anywhere.

And many important nocturnal dreams are dreamed to no purpose, because people shake them off in the morning. The hustle of life calls, and there is no time to sit down and think whether there was a message in the dream. A pity, because there often is a message and it can change a whole day because it often refers to the day that is about the begin.

With many people the area of prayer and meditation remains untilled because they have never learned that it is possible to turn inwards. They have become so fascinated by their outer senses that their inner world is just a vague place of shadows. What happens then? Really important abilities, such as those that express themselves through prayer, meditation and dreams, are not used. The people who daydream are really just generating nice sensations, they are just eating psychic chocolate creams. Nice, but it leads to tooth decay. In this case, it would be the decay of very important abilities.

What I am pleading for is that once more we consciously make use of these forces and fortunately we see nowadays that the interest of the new generation is turned more and more to these inner regions.

There is an important parallel between physical and psychic sources of energy as regards the way they are emerging in our time.

In the new prayer groups, in the new interest taken in meditation and dreams, we see that people are really consciously striving to tap these new sources of energy. The inexhaustible stream of psychic energy of which still far too much is allowed to flow away, is already being channelled and used in several places.

And thus we also see that the force of gravity, which lies within everyone's reach and that also flows away unused, is waiting only for the machines which will deliver to us this inexhaustible and clean source of power.

But we will have to work hard for both streams of energy, the spiritual and the mundane.

I have just said that psychic energy flows away in daydreams. But meditative energy also has many good opportunities for leaking away.

Meditation is the emptying of the mind. Not thinking, but totally focussed and aware. Well, a caricature of this situation comes into being when we drive very fast along a highway. Anybody doing that finds himself in a kind of unconscious meditation. In the same way as daydreams are chocolate creams, driving fast is psychic chewing gum.

There is also such a thing as imitation prayer. What is worship? Your total submission to the above. What is the present caricature of prayer? Watching television or video recordings in total fascination, or playing computer games. Such a person is really just sucking fruit gums.

No, the intention is that we ponder on our dreams, that we sharply analyse our daydreams so as to get to know ourselves, that we do not silence our mind by drugging it with speed but that we sit down and simply remain lucid. That we direct our adoration to Him Who must be adored.

Understand that I have nothing against television, video recordings and computer games. Nor have I anything against speed. I only want to make plain that where these have enslaved, they have replaced meditation and prayer, so understanding has really been switched off. And as I said, I am not pleading for disconnection of understanding but would advise you to take in new ideas from the creative regions and allow those to filter through the sieve of intelligence.

That is in fact in direct contrast to those who try to enlarge their awareness by the use of drugs. Drugs do indeed give you a greatly increased power of imagination but at the same time they disconnect the critical appraisal of your own images. In this manner you are reduced to a cow chewing its cud or the lotus eater from the Voyages of Odysseus. That does not get us anywhere. The use of drugs is masturbation of one's creative abilities and does not deliver what is required. But a creative ability that goes through the sieve of reason and is joined to action, yes, that can literally move mountains.

I suspect that in these times it could well be easier to make contact with heaven than for instance in the previous century. And now I must refer to an idea that is not mine but that I do subscribe to, which is that the distance from heaven to earth is not a constant but varies from time to time. Of course it is strange to be using a word like distance when at least one of the two items between which we are measuring distance is of a spiritual nature. One must therefore take this more in a psychological sense.

The term psychological distance is now quite familiar and ordinary, everyday usage. Just listen to the following sentences:

'That idea is far out.'

'She had a somewhat distant manner.'

'I feel that we have drifted apart these last few months.'
These are the sort of distances I am talking about.

There are times when heaven is above and earth is beneath and everyone, to coin a phrase, goes his own way. 'God's in His heaven and all's right with the world' was a well-known saying at the peak of the British Empire.

It seems to me that there was a great distance between heaven and earth in the middle of the previous century. During the first half of the nineteenth century Hildebrand wrote his 'Camera Obscura'. It is a famous Dutch book and it paints an exact picture of those days. Every Dutch school child is familiar with the characters in this book, and near to where I live they have been portrayed by a well-known sculptor and put in a famous park mentioned in this book.

One scene in the 'Camera Obscura' takes place just before the feast of St Nicholas, when all Dutch people give each other presents and specially written poems. At the local baker a lot of ladies who fancy themselves, gather together to paint the typical enormous Dutch biscuits baked in the shape of peasant lovers. Everything takes place in an absolutely relaxed atmosphere of bourgeois gentility; no-one has heard of the word haste, and the world has no greater mysteries than what is to be served for supper. It would be quite unthinkable that during such a festive gathering an angel would suddenly appear. And mind you, the 'Camera Obscura' is a most exact description of the Netherlands in the middle of the last century.

Just contrast this book with another that paints a picture of the middle of our own century — Paul Gallico's 'Snow Goose'. The 'Camera Obscura' is from 1839. The 'Snow Goose' is set during the battle at Dunkirk in 1940, 100 years later. But in the 'Snow Goose' you hear as it were the rushing of angel wings.

Heaven appears to be approaching earth in this century and with such acceleration that it is quite different from all other times when a similar thing was happening. There have been times like that, and I will come back to that later on.

But what we are now experiencing is something so radical that I cannot point to any historical period during which the same thing happened. It is as if heaven and earth are on a collision course.

An aside to those who do not know what a collision course is: if two ships follow imaginary linear courses and those lines cross somewhere and the speed of these ships is such that they will both arrive at the intersection of those two lines at the same time, one talks about a collision course. In open water there is a simple trick to find out if you are on a collision course with another ship. Simply look at the bank behind that other ship. If that ship, compared to the bank behind, seems to be advancing, it will pass in front of you. If instead the bank appears to be moving forwards, so that it seems as if the ship is moving backwards, then that ship will pass behind you. If the bank lies still behind the other ship, then you are on a collision course and if you continue you will undoubtedly hit each other. At sea, where there is no fixed coast as background, this trick does not work.

Unfortunately we cannot apply a similar trick to the courses of heaven and earth. Heaven is not visible to us, let alone the background against which heaven could be seen to move.

Suppose that my statement that we are on a collision course with heaven is correct. What can we expect?

I must now clarify my image of the two ships a little. The two ships are sailing through the night. The celestial ship is all lit up and is equipped with powerful searchlights. The terrestrial ship has only a small navigation light on top of the mast. As the two ships approach each other nearer and nearer, the terrestrial ship is gradually lit up more and more. And the consequences of this would be that what we call the unperceivable world will break through more and more in man's consciousness. First in an individual, then with more people and finally by the thousand at the same time, just as already some thousands of people simultaneously observe UFOs.

But we can also assume that where the light of the celestial ship falls on the terrestrial ship, the shadows cast by the rigging will get ever stronger.

Let us go a little further into both the light breaking through and the shadows getting stronger.

As far as the light breaking through is concerned, the Swedish enquiry and my own survey speak volumes. We are dealing here with a phenomenon that we ought to take very seriously. Out of my random 400 people there are at least ninety-nine who have experienced some form of extra-sensory perception. The Swedish enquiry elicited a stream of letters.

Contact with heaven appears to be already quite intense, without us even realising it. It is, however, anxiously kept quiet.

And as far as the shadows that are cast getting stronger, it is clear that besides heaven, hell is also breaking through. Weapons are available of such frightfulness that they are so far beyond human powers of imagination that people talk of them in the careless way one talks of ordinary old-fashioned cannons. Or again, people take up new forms of crime the equal of which is not known in human history, as for instance, terrorism. In times gone by, there was indeed terrorism, but that was committed against what was seen to be the enemy. Currently, terrorism is literally hell let loose on earth. A hellish device explodes in the middle of a market with cheerful shoppers or perhaps during a friendly parade in an English park.

Sometimes I think, 'This is so awful that even Satan could learn something new.'

And yet . . . that form of terrorism is the fiery devil. It is carried out by brutal fanatics, mostly psychopathically degenerate characters.

242

Much worse is the frigid devil. The one who murders out of scientific curiosity. The doctor in a State mental hospital injects dissidents with a substance that causes insanity and then examines the result with cool interest. The scientist who uses the living foetus for 'interesting' experiments and then strokes his children's hair when he comes home. The psychologist who, using a sophisticated psychological system of torture with frightful punishment and tiny rewards, turns his political opponent into a slavish fellow traveller.

These are the new criminals of the twentieth century, incredibly frightening people because what they do leaves them completely cold. How right was Dante to depict Hell's inner circle as a clump of ice:

'The emperor of the sorrowful realm was there,

Out of the girding ice he stood breast-high . . .'

If heaven and earth lie on a collision course, you can see that the consequence is that the people on this earth divide themselves spiritually. The ones like devils become ever more satanic, the angelic ones become more as man is meant to be — warm and friendly.

Even fewer people remain who do not belong to one of the two sides.

One man will vote in his heart for one side, the other in his heart for the other. A silent majority does not exist.

Have there been other times when heaven and earth approached each other so closely that the one broke through violently into the other?

Our thoughts go immediately to the time of the Exodus. Tremendous miracles took place in Egypt; the ten plagues and later on the even greater wonder of the journey through the Red Sea and the giving of the Law on Mount Sinai.

Just before the Exodus there was terrible oppression of a whole people and the murder of little boys. Heaven and hell were visible simultaneously then, too.

However, on a planetary scale this was just a grazing shot that took place mainly in Egypt. I say mainly, because Velikovsky has shown good grounds for maintaining his opinion that important events took place elsewhere in the world at the same time.

But this time it looks as if we are approaching a head-on collision.

We are threatened by something other than an atomic war. What is hanging over our heads is a breakthrough of the unperceived world.

One of these signs is the exceptionally interesting development which has arisen in the research on the problem of death. The great taboo was broken. People like Elisabeth Kubler Ross and other investigators have been actively engaged in studying the process of dying and naturally encountered that which happens after death. They discovered that death is not the end of consciousness but a breaking through. Mankind has always known this but the knowledge was lost with the advent of materialism. And it is now coming back in an irresistable flood.

Another sign of the heavenly breakthrough is the increasing number of people with psychic disturbances. The calm, regular radio broadcasts of normal consciousness are continually disturbed in those people by worlds trying to break through. And because they have not been prepared they become frightened, depressed, paranoid and start acting strangely. You see this happening to young people especially. The number of students needing psychological help is tremendously large. And that is in striking contrast to thirty-five years ago when I was a student myself. And that was in fact a generation which emerged straight out of the war.

Because of the pressure of heaven coming our way, the human soul is on the point of bursting. Many women are sharply aware of this. They are the ones who do not dare to come out into the street. They feel greatly threatened in shops, in squares and streets or in a bus.

And if you ask them what scares them so much, they tell you that they are terrified of fainting or even dropping dead. That is nothing but the fear that the other world will break through at some unexpected moment. They may think that the threat comes from the outside, but in reality it is lurking in a totally unsuspected direction, from the 'inside' of life.

Should we really be afraid of a head-on collision with heaven? I am of two minds, yes and no, which one really depends on our attitude. We must realise that heaven has good intentions towards us but that we should be afraid of the shadows which the approaching light can call up in us and other people. This paradoxical situation that the approach of light increases the danger of people having bizarre reactions, makes the situation very explosive. On top of that, there are always people who prefer to belong to darkness rather than to light. Who want to wage war against it. Who try to change the planet quickly before the light breaks through definitively. To change it into a smoking desert or a grave for the billions. So that the eventual breakthrough of heaven will not have a living soul to welcome it. For if one thing is clear in these times it is the haste of hell.

The wicked almost stumble over their own feet in their haste to corrupt this world totally. That is why murder is no longer perpetrated these days in the customary manner. Well, of course, it still happens, but it is not the speciality of the twentieth century. The speciality of this century is genocide. The elimination of a complete people as if we are dealing with a plague of rabbits. This is done on a small scale to the Indians in the Amazon area, and on a large scale by the Russians in Afghanistan.

The wicked are in a hurry. Nobody but the hard, the bitter and the frigid are allowed to survive. The friendly, the people involved with nature and the people rooted in tradition have to be eradicted root and branch.

With this, the task of every person of good will is clear, in the latter half of the twentieth century. Head touches tail, this is the exact task laid on man when he was still in paradise. There in the Garden of Eden he was told that he must both dress and keep the garden.

The word 'dress' is a translation of the Hebrew word 'awoda'. It means working it, in the sense of serving it. If someone knows how to keep a small piece of this earth from being poisoned, even if it is his own garden, then he is practising awoda in our time.

If someone devotes himself to achieving a clean environment in his city, county or state, or in the ocean that surrounds us, then it is awoda. This awoda is not an unattainable ideal, it is a practical possibility for everyone. But the one who works on his own soul to keep it clean is also busy with awoda.

We know nowadays that a serious illness such as cancer can sometimes be caused by deep resentments left in the soul against our parents, teachers and guardians. Or because anger is festering in our hidden depths where no-one can see it, very often not even the person cherishing this anger and who keeps saying to himself that everything in the garden is lovely. Such a person has to find out that hatred still exists in his life. Sometimes the hated person is still alive and then the anger and rage are continuously suppressed. As one of my patients said, 'The breast I lost I offered on my mother's altar.'

If such a person can really discover that a poisonous plant is growing in his soul, then a simple exercise will already make a difference. The exercise in which you sit down every day for a moment and imagine that something delightful, something really nice and cheerful happens to the one against whom you nurse a grudge. Then the grudge and the

246

hatred gradually evaporate and you will even rejoice in the happiness you wish the other. That too is awoda, and is within everyone's reach. We are not offered unattainable goals.

It is wrong to think that the problems appearing on earth are too big for us, that we cannot take them on any more. The problems we see on a planetary scale are no different from the ones we see in everyday life to a much smaller degree. And there, in your own soul and your own garden, awoda starts. There the cleansing of this dirtied planet begins. And if enough people occupy themselves with this, then it all adds up. Then something is changed in the Creative Heaven and you see it returning to earth some time later with positive repercussions.

The opposite of the Club of Rome's prophecies of doom can happen. And everyone can 'take that trick'. Dutch people are always wondering whether they can take a metaphorical trick in the bridge game that is life. Well, the cards that can save the planet lie in your own hands.

The second task given to man is to keep. That is the translation of the Hebrew word 'shamer'.

The ancient commentary says that this means man keeping the wild animals at a distance.

Well now, you will say, there are hardly any wild animals left in our world. At the most a few in wildlife parks and in zoos.

That is true, but we have been given dangerous ones instead. Because of the brutal encroachment of hell, everyone who wishes the best for this planet is involved with the fight. That cannot possibly be avoided. If it is then you must seriously ask yourself if you are doing the right thing.

Whether you are fighting against the dumping of atomic waste in your county, against the cruise missile in your country, against political indoctrination of your children or against your own hatred, your own cowardice, your own egoism, your own mortally dangerous inclination to conform because otherwise you would not be liked by people, fighting is something all of us will have to do in this century. Sitting on the fence will become less and less possible.

There is one quality which will be decisive in the coming ten years, and that is moral courage.

'Let the weak say, I am strong.' (Joel 3, verse 10)

And indeed a lot of courage is needed nowadays not to howl along with the wolves of the forest. To have the courage to allow oneself to be considered a little eccentric, to be unpopular.

This planet is a beleaguered fortress, the enemy is mighty and rushes forward irresistably. But relief is at hand.

These relief troops come from a totally unexpected quarter. A single soldier to these relief troops is enough to defeat a whole enemy division.

But they have not arrived as yet. Only their scouts are making contact with the vanguard of those of good will to all people. We must hold on just a little longer in the gathering darkness. Just at this moment we must not lose hope, just now we must display an indestructible optimism.

Let everyone of good will do his utmost to dress and keep the little bit of planet that he is allotted. Rescue is just round the corner.

What will that rescue look like?

Let us start with an easy example. The greatest current threat in the outer world — the atom bomb.

These fiendish contraptions cannot be dismantled from the outside. But let us go a little deeper into the matter. What is an atom? It is whirl.

Not a whirl of matter but a whirl of force, a force that breaks through from the invisible world to our own and gives form to that which we call matter. That matter which is created every moment from the invisible world.

We have said earlier that behind the physical whirl of what we call atoms, a spiritual whirl is hidden, caused by the high angel hierarchy known as ophanim or Thrones. Just imagine that one such exalted angel of the order of ophanim or wheels were to appear here on earth and direct his gaze on the underground silo in Siberia where a rocket with a multiple atomic warhead lies waiting to be launched as a hellish firework against the west and with one blow destroy Amsterdam, Rotterdam, Utrecht, Den Helder, Den Haag, Arnhem, Eindhoven, Breda, Enschede and Leeuwarden.

Just one jab of the button separates us from this event. Let us not try to suppress or imagine that it will not really happen. Communist theory knows nothing of moral principles, it is simply opportunist. If the high command says at a given moment that it is time to press the button, then the button is duly pressed and those ten cities will vanish along with all their inhabitants within twenty minutes.

But right now we have the angel from the order of ophanim standing there. And just at the moment that the roof of the silo starts opening and the rocket rises into the sky (angels always wait till the last possible moment), the angel regards that instrument from hell. And at that precise moment he changes the inner structure of all the atoms that are on their way to loose destruction. That is not really difficult for that particular angel since he is the one who gives life to all atoms. The men firing off the rocket would notice nothing, but inside such a multiple H-bomb a cavity would have been created, filled with just a little helium gas.

Is that just what we call 'wishful thinking'? Making the wish the father of the thought? Is it unrealistic perhaps?

Do not forget that once previously such a disdained man walked the earth. He was called Noah and he built a boat in the middle of dry land. And just think of the King of England in World War 2 who, when the whole British expeditionary force was threatened with destruction at Dunkirk, declared that day a national day of prayer. Britain fell as one man on its knees and what is known as the 'miracle of Dunkirk' took place. Instead of only one tenth part of the army that was expected to return nine-tenths came home safely.

Can we not borrow some of this sort of foolishness that Noah and King George VI had in such generous measure? May we not trust that if we have 'dressed' and 'kept' our own piece of soil and prayed for deliverance that the final bursting out of hell will be kept back? May we not return to a 'simple' way of thinking and joyfully await a miracle?

I think we can and we may. Neither you nor I can in any way change the ever growing American and Russian arsenals of rockets. We are really not strong enough. Let us then do something totally different.

Let us take measures to prepare a feast for gathering the ophanim, the wheels. Let us try to obtain help from the angels who stand above the atoms.

It is absolutely unnecessary for today's youth to be pessimistic about their future. A tremendous adventure awaits them. That adventure is as great as the search for the Holy Grail in the time of King Arthur and his Round Table.

There is only one difficulty, and it is that adventure does not lie primarily in the outer world in our time but in the inner world. This is on the border between heaven and earth where encounters with angels take place.

Yes, naturally you fight also in this outer world against dirt and injustice, but to everyone who does this in the twentieth century there comes a moment when he realises that he is fighting against gigantic spiritual forces, invisible giants. You know that you urgently need help from this same invisible world because otherwise you will not be able to make it.

Cannot those invisible forces that attack us be immediately destroyed by the angels? If they are so powerful, what on earth do they need us for?

Yes, I think that is quite a mystery.

We products of a welfare state are so used to being served our every wish that we forget that the whole struggle is about us. Avoiding this confrontation is inviting disaster. Let me give an example.

Little Peter has to take an arithmetic test at school and he does not want to, so he plays truant. Does it really get us anywhere if his teacher does the sums? Of course not.

It is the same with humanity. We are here to learn something essential, and that is love and wisdom. That is possible only through strife and suffering. If those things did not exist down here, then this would be a school for jellyfish. Because free will is the hallmark of heaven, just as violence is the hallmark of hell, a lot of courage is required to take up with heaven, perhaps more than anything else because people will laugh at you.

Searching for the Kingdom of God does not spoil a person of this earth with honour but with ridicule.

Oranges or lemons, which will you choose?

We all have to choose sides if we are to enter the Kingdom of Heaven, or Angel-land. However, in order to enter we must have with us the key to that kingdom. And I believe that the materialism of the last century has broken that key, and the greed of this century has lost the pieces.

Is there someone who can find these pieces and mend them? Is it for sale in a supermarket?

No, just look at the label. Something that is full of preservatives, artificial colouring and monosodium glutamate is in no way going to be the key to heaven. Rather, it is the key to a malignant growth.

Can I find the key with a guru? Your chances are slim. The one who opens up shop by the side of the road is a businessman, and the one who works his wonders quietly is never found.

Does the Church hand over the key? The Church may talk about the key, but it does not hand it over. Well, where am I

17 Rembrandt: Christ on the Mount of Olives:
'And there appeared an angel unto Him from
heaven, strengthening Him.'

going to find the key? In this crazy world you can fly to the other side of the globe, can buy a house, can have a heart transplant and yet be unable to obtain a key to the Kingdom of Heaven.

I shall show you the only person who can get this key for you. Go to your bedroom and shut the door. Look into the mirror. Look, there stands the only figure that can look for and find the key to the kingdom of the angels. No-one can do it for you. Many would like to give you a helping hand, but each person must walk his own road, must do his own work. There is no other.

The welfare state has made 'spiritual lazybones' of us all. We are prepared to work hard in order to save up for a holiday but we feel insulted if someone says we must work hard for the Kingdom of God.

Surely Jesus has done all that for us already? Why should we worry?

No, it is not as easy as that. It is true that Jesus banged open the door which had been closed for so long.

But you, and no-one else, will have to walk the road to the gates that were pushed open. When someone walks that road he is met by angels.

How do we walk that road? And how intensely do we treat the path?

There is an old story about the time Israel stood before the Red Sea. Behind them was Pharoah's army. In front of them the sea. This legend is about one man, called Nachson, who took the command of God and His promises absolutely seriously. He said, 'If God wants us to go on, then we go on!' And he walked straight into the water. Everyone thought him mad, but he walked in further and further, steadfastly trusting in God.

Finally the waters closed over his head and everyone said, 'That is what comes of it, there is such a thing as trusting too much.'

And at precisely that moment when Nachson nearly drowned, the sea split into twelve corridors, it congealed like crystal and the twelve tribes of Israel passed through the corridors to the other side.

That is how mad a person has to be in his trust. For then miracles take place. Then God sends His servants and man is helped in the most remarkable ways.

In the near future we shall need such people. As the times get darker, people like Nachson must arise who, despite everything, dare to remain optimistic.

Perhaps you are such a person.

God bless you!

Bibliography

The Apocryphal New Testament Clarendon Press

Floris B. Bakels, *Uitzicht, De lessen van Nacht und Nebel*, Elsevier, Amsterdam/Brussels

R. Boon, *Over de goede engelen of de ontmaskering van een pedant geloof* Boekencentrum, Den Haag

E. W. Bullinger, *The Witness of the Stars* Lamp Press, London

Nigel Calder, *The comet is coming* Penguin Books

Fritjof Capra, *The Tao of Physics* Fontana/Collins, London

Carole Carlson, *Corrie ten Boom, her life, her faith* Fleming H. Revell Company, New Jersey

Carlos Castaneda, *The teachings of Don Juan* Penguin Books

R. H. Charles, *The Book of Enoch* SPCK, London

Philip Chancellor, *Handboek voor de bloesemtherapie van dr. Bach* Ankh-Hermes, Deventer

Erich von Däniken, *Waren de goden kosmonauten?* Ankh-Hermes, Deventer

Dante Alighieri, *De goddelijke komedie* Wereldbibliotheek, Amsterdam

Ann Faraday, *Dream Power* Hodder and Stoughton, London

Paul Gallico, *The Snow Goose* Michael Joseph Ltd., London

Billy Graham, *Angels, God's secret agents* Hodder & Stoughton, London

Myrna Grant, *Vanya* Gideon, Hoornaar

Guideposts (March and May '82, April '83) Carmel, New York

Gunnar Hillerdal/Berndt Gustafsson, *Sie erlebten Christus* Die Pforte, Basel

Charles F. Hunter, *Angels on Assignment* Hunter Books

Robert Jungk, *De atoomstaat* Elsevier, Amsterdam/Brussels

Ken Keyes, *The Hundreth Monkey* Vision Books, Kentucky

Willem Koppejan/Helene van Woelderen, *J. Bernard Nicklin* Real Israel Press, Glastonbury/Den Haag

B. Kristensen, J. E. de Vries e.a., *Sensitivity-training . . . en hoe verder?* Buijten & Schipperheijn, Amsterdam

Elisabeth Kübler Ross, *Lessen voor levenden* Ambo, Bilthoven

Kathryn Kuhlman, *Ik geloof in wonderen* Gideon, Hoornaar

Selma Lagerlof, *Nils Holgersson* Becht, Amsterdam

Lawrence Le Shan, *How to Meditate* Turnstone Press, Northamptonshire

Jakob Lorber, *Das grosze Evangelium Johannis* Lorder Verlag, Bietigheim

D. McNutt, *Healing* Notra Dame, Indianna

Anthony Mertens, *Sterke verhalen* Spectrum, De Meern

Rudolf Meyer, *De mens en zijn engel* Christofoor, Zeist

Czeslaw Milosz, *The captive mind* Vintage Books, Random House, New York

T. Henry Moray, *The sea of energy in which the earth floats* Cosray

Research Institute, Salt Lake City

Maurice Nicoll, *Psychological Commentaries on the Teaching of G. I. Gurdjieff and P. D. Ouspensky* Vincent Stuart, London

Hans A. Nieper, *Revolution in Technik, Medizin, Gesellschaft* Illmer Verlag, Hannover

P. D. Ouspensky, *A New Model of the Universe* Routledge and Kegan

Rien Poortvliet/Wil Huysen, *Leven en werken van de kabouter* Van Holkema & Warendorf, Bussum

Lydia Prince, *Appointment in Jerusalem* Flemings H. Revell, Old Tappan, New Jersey

Adolf Schneider/Hubert Malthaner, *UFO-fotoboek* Ankh-Hermes, Deventer

Hans W. Schroeder, *De hemelse hiërarchieën. Rangorde en verscheidenheid* Christofoor, Zeist

Theodor Schwenk, *Das sensibele Chaos* Freies Geistesleben, Stuttgart

Joy Snell, *The Ministry of Angels* The greater world association, London

Rupert Sheldrake, *A new science of Life* Blond & Briggs, London

Rudolf Steiner, *Hoe werken de engelen in ons astraallichaam* Vrij Geestesleven, Zeist

Rudolf Steiner, *Die Geheimwissenschaft im Umriss* Goetheanum, Dornach

O. Carl Simonton/Stephanie Matthews-Somonton/James Creighton, *Op weg naar herstel* Intro, Nijkerk

W. P. Theunissen, *Engelen. Overwegingen in beelden en teksten* Berghaar Verlag

Chriet Titulaer, *De mens in de ruimte* Elsevier, Amsterdam

J. R. R. Tolkien, *The Lord of the Rings* George Allen & Unwin Ltd., London

Mellie Uyldert, *De verborgen schat in het kinderspel* De Driehoek, Amsterdam

Immanuel Velikovsky, *Werelden in botsing* Ankh-Hermes, Deventer

W. F. Veltman, *Over de hemelse hiërarchieën* Studiecentrum voor antroposophie

A. C. Vreeburg, *Preek in de kerk van de Hl. Lodewijk*, Leiden

Alan Watts, *The Way of Zen* Pantheon Books, New York

Friedrich Weinreb, *Ik die verborgen ben* Servire, Katwijk

Friedrich Weinreb, *Begegnungen mit Engeln und Menschen* (cursussen 1964 – 1965, 1965 – 1967, 1967 – 1968) Origo Verlag, Zürich

Clément A. Wertheim Aymès, *Die Bildersprache des Hieronymus Bosch* Van Goor & Zn., Den Haag

Julien Weverbergh, *UFO's in het verleden* Ankh-Hermes, Deventer

Peter Wilson, *Angels* Thames and Hudson, London

Z'ev Ben Shimon HaLevi, *Tree of Life* Rider & Company, London